What We

What We Are Fighting For

A Radical Collective Manifesto

Edited by
Federico Campagna
and
Emanuele Campiglio

PlutoPress
www.plutobooks.com

First published 2012 by Pluto Press
345 Archway Road, London N6 5AA

www.plutobooks.com

Distributed in the United States of America exclusively by
Palgrave Macmillan, a division of St. Martin's Press LLC,
175 Fifth Avenue, New York, NY 10010

British Library Cataloguing in Publication Data
A catalogue record for this book is available from the British Library

ISBN   978 0 7453 3286 4   Hardback
ISBN   978 0 7453 3285 7   Paperback
ISBN   978 1 8496 4761 8   PDF eBook
ISBN   978 1 8496 4763 2   Kindle eBook
ISBN   978 1 8496 4762 5   EPUB eBook

Library of Congress Cataloging in Publication Data applied for

This book is printed on paper suitable for recycling and made from fully
managed and sustained forest sources. Logging, pulping and manufacturing
processes are expected to conform to the environmental standards of the
country of origin.

10   9   8   7   6   5   4   3   2   1

Designed and produced for Pluto Press by Chase Publishing Services Ltd
Typeset from disk by Stanford DTP Services, Northampton, England
Simultaneously printed digitally by CPI Antony Rowe, Chippenham, UK and
Edwards Bros in the United States of America

Contents

Acknowledgements

The editors would like to thank all the contributors to this volume, David Castle and the staff at Pluto Press, Charlotte Bonham-Carter and Gemma Tortella at the ICA, London. Thanks to Deterritorial Support Group for the artwork on the cover.

Federico Campagna would also like to thank Anna Galkina, for her invaluable and loving help, and Luciano, Nellina and Elisabetta Campagna, for their constant support. Thanks also to Franco Berardi Bifo, Sara Brouwer, Mark Fisher, Alex Foti, Adam Haggerty, Henry Hartley, Adelita Husni-Bey, Richard John Jones, Alessio Kolioulis, Yari Lanci, Huw Lemmey, Paolo Mossetti, Michael Oswell, Tania Palmieri, Manlio Poltronieri, Robert Prouse, Alessandra Sciurba, Kika Sroka-Miller for being such wonderful friends and, indeed, comrades.

Federico would like to dedicate this volume to all those who are escaping from a police siren.

Preface
Exodus Without Promised Land

Christian Marazzi

I must make some preliminary remarks: I am not used to thinking in terms of 'alternative economics' and even less in terms of utopias, especially when the issue at stake is that of the economic organisation of life after liberalism. Considering the state of things in neoliberal financial capitalism, I believe that the recent waves of struggles for democracy and freedom, and against the exploitation of the social workforce, already *in themselves* prefigure alternative ways of life. They are a 'here and now' which, on the one hand, points at possible ways out of neoliberal capitalism while, on the other, is marked by a strange in-actuality, as if it were a case of an infinite transition, a process with no end, an exodus without promised land. It is as we were *forced* to resist, to say no to the continuous attacks waged by capital – in particular of financial capital – against our livelihoods, while not being able to develop methods of struggle which are affirmative, aggregative and constitutive of permanent organisations of autonomous, free and democratic life.

Working conditions have rarely been more degrading, tiring and empty of satisfaction than they are today – and, I fear, will be in the near future. Never more so than today, the conditions of our material life are subject to forces that we can no longer control, other than with a great effort of abstraction. It is the case with the financial crises that have periodically interrupted the process of capitalist accumulation for the last 30 years.

Nonetheless, within this apparent fragmentation of the front of struggle, within this process of singularisation and localisation of the resistances against financial capital, we cannot deny that something alternative and parallel is growing. This something has been called 'the commons', and indeed they are the commons that are working in the background of the multiple forms of resistance. These commons, as was the case with land at the time of primitive accumulation, these sets of 'positive externalities' produced within capitalism, are the grounds on which we have to invent and promote affirmative struggles, to institute alternative ways of life, even at the cost of pure experimentation and partiality.

These commons are those parts of the unrecognised and unremunerated production of wealth which have made it possible for capital to develop without wealth redistribution, and for profits to grow systematically without any similar growth in investments in instrumental goods, salaries and occupations. The commons of intersubjective languages, of cooperation and the sharing of knowledge, the commons of affections, of friendship and relational action, have for a long time been the 'virgin land' appropriated by capital through its development of financial bubbles, its destruction and concentration of wealth, and its de-structuring of parallel economies (the economies of the commons) without any restructuring of the conditions of material life.

This is what the financialisation of economy is all about: the production of wealth through the commons, the creation of financial revenues in order to monetarise a mass of surplus-value (which is cognitive in a broad sense) for which there is no other place in an economy based on wage relationships. Finance is, so to speak, the 'bad commons' par excellence, the 'purest form of interaction', as Simmel defined it, in which money is the pure representation of the relationship humans have with the world, 'which can only be grasped in single and concrete instances, yet only really conceived when the singular becomes the embodiment of the living mental process which interweaves all singularities and, in this fashion, creates reality.'[1]

These 'financial commons' are the debt economy which is transversal to the whole of the social structure, from the investors to the consumers, to the workers faced by low salaries, intermittent precarity and unemployment. Within the debt economy, we have seen financial capital growing, we have seen the work of its *dispositif de captation* of the cognitive surplus-value produced by the actions of the commons, by the social networks of cooperation and of relationship. Within the debt economy, we have seen the growth of access to the network society, the putting-to-work of the social labour force, of its entire life. But we have also seen that the process of inclusion inevitably involves also its reverse, the process of exclusion which characterises financial crises and the bursting of the bubbles.

Within this cycle of expansion/inclusion/exclusion, within this on-off process of privatisation of the commons, one of the ways of turning what we experience and live into something positive is the overturning of debt into basic income. To reclaim the right to bankruptcy, the right to transform private debts into social income – this is, I believe, a good way of standing up to financial capitalism and the violence of its logic of acquisition of the commons.

The other path of affirmative struggle has to do with reclaiming life-time. To create employment through the redistribution of the excessive labour of those already at work, to reduce the time of work by raising the level of employment, and to do so in the environmentally sustainable sectors. This objective is at the same time reformist and revolutionary, in the sense that it places itself within a transformation which is necessary to capitalism, but that simultaneously poses the issue of reclaiming life and the quality of life as an elsewhere which has to be reached here and now.

After years of systematic destruction of the welfare state through tax cuts and cuts to public spending in line with the principle of 'starving the beast', the time has come to reaffirm the aim of a welfare of the commons, or, better, of a welfare of cognitive freedom. Within the frame of today's capitalism, the trend is towards putting every single human activity to profit. Capital is ready to pay for some of these activities, even to transform a billion people into busy 'happiness workers', as long as the wage-isation of the *bios* and of all cognitive and affective activities is matched by an equally all-pervasive marketisation of the brain. I am thinking, for example, of Facebook and their idea of paying 10 cents to any user prepared to watch an advertising video to the end. It is on this terrain that we must mobilise, on the one hand reclaiming income as remuneration of the productive activity of the *bios*, but on the other creating laboratories of liberation of the mind, physical places of mental liberation.

During the last few years I had direct experience of a struggle within the railway industry. Strike, occupation, mobilisation of the entire local community, institution of a place of socialisation of life. I have seen an industry-specific struggle producing society, moments of exchange, affects, relationships, on all levels, from the physical to the internet. The institution of the commons and its self-organisation have been possible thanks to the enduring occupation of a physical space. Only through the concreteness and the physicality of the struggle and of its organisational forms is it possible to create the commons, to liberate their voices and to make them explicit. During these months of struggle, lost knowledge has emerged, and with it also relational webs as-yet-unknown, management skills for complex productive processes which were close to pure self-organisation. Then, it all ended. Not really, as some of us still carry on that struggle, seemingly endless, in which the promised land always seems to move further away. And yet, we don't feel alone, even if we are.

NOTE

1. Georg Simmel, *The Philosophy of Money* (Routledge, 2005), p. 128.

Notes on Contributors

Michael Albert is co-founder of *ZNet*, *ZMagazine*, South End Press and of the International Organization for a Participatory Society. Among his books are *Parecon* (Verso, 2002) and *Realizing Hope* (Zed Books, 2008).

Milford Bateman is a freelance consultant on local economic development policy and visiting professor of economics at Juraj Dobrila University at Pula in Croatia. He is the author of *Why Doesn't Microfinance Work?* (Zed Books, 2010).

Franco Berardi Bifo is Professor of Social History of Communication at Accademia di Belle Arti, Milan, and co-founder of SCEPSI, European School of Social Imagination. Among his books are *Precarious Rhapsody* (Autonomedia, 2009), *The Soul at Work* (Semiotext(e) 2010) and *After the Future* (AK Press, 2011).

Federico Campagna is co-founder of the online journal *Through Europe* and editor of *Canone Bifido* (Il Saggiatore, 2013).

Shaun Chamberlin is co-founder of Transition Town Kingston, a council member of the World Development Movement and Development Director for TEQs. He is author of *The Transition Timeline* (Green Books, 2009).

Zillah Eisenstein is a professor at the Department of Politics at Ithaca University, New York. Among her books are *Against Empire* (Zed Books, 2004), *Sexual Decoys* (Zed Books, 2007) and *The Audacity of Races and Genders* (Zed Books, 2009).

Mark Fisher is a writer for *Sight and Sound*, *Film Quarterly* and *The Wire* and blogger K-Punk. He is author of *Capitalist Realism* (Zero Books, 2009).

David Graeber is Reader in Anthropology at Goldsmiths, University of London. Among his books are *Fragments of an Anarchist Anthropology* (Prickly Paradigm, 2004), *Direct Action* (AK Press, 2009) and *Debt* (Melville House, 2011).

Peter Hallward is Professor of Modern European Philosophy at Kingston University, a member of the *Radical Philosophy* editorial collective and contributing editor to *Angelaki*. Among his books are *Out of This World* (Verso, 2006) and *Damming the Flood* (Verso, 2011).

Dan Hind is a journalist at Al Jazeera and the author of *The Threat to Reason* (Verso, 2007), *The Return of the Public* (Verso, 2011) and *Common Sense* (various publishers, 2012).

Owen Jones is a journalist at the *Independent* and the author of *Chavs* (Verso, 2011).

Christian Marazzi is Director of Socio-Economic Research at the Scuola Universitaria della Svizzera Italiana. Among his books are *Capital and Affects* (Semiotext(e) 2011), *The Violence of Financial Capitalism* (Semiotext(e) 2011) and *Capital and Language* (Semiotext(e) 2008).

Saul Newman is Reader in Political Theory at Goldsmiths, University of London. Among his books are *From Bakunin to Lacan* (Lexington Books, 2009), *The Politics of Postanarchism* (EUP, 2011) and *Max Stirner* (Palgrave Macmillan, 2011).

Ann Pettifor is Director of PRIME Policy Research in Macroeconomics and a fellow of the New Economics Foundation, London. Among her books are *The Real World Economic Outlook* (Palgrave Macmillan, 2003) and *The Coming First World Debt Crisis* (Palgrave Macmillan, 2006).

Nina Power is Senior Lecturer in Philosophy at Roehampton University, Lecturer in Critical Writing on Art and Design at Royal College of Art and a journalist for the *Guardian*. She is the author of *One Dimensional Woman* (Zero Books, 2009).

Richard Seymour is a journalist for the *Guardian* and blogger at Lenin's Tomb. He is the author of *The Liberal Defence of Murder* (Verso, 2008) and *The Meaning of David Cameron* (Zero Books 2010).

Marina Sitrin is a lawyer, activist and organiser, and the author of *Horizontalism* (AK Press, 2006), *Everyday Revolutions* (Zed Books, 2012) and *They Can't Represent US!* (Verso, 2013).

Mark J. Smith is a senior lecturer in Politics and International Studies at the Open University. He is co-author of *Environment and Citizenship* (Zed Books, 2008) and *Responsible Politics* (Palgrave Macmillan, 2013).

South London Solidarity Federation are part of the Solidarity Federation, a federation of groups and individuals across England, Scotland & Wales committed to building a non-hierarchical, anti-authoritarian solidarity movement.

Alberto Toscano is Senior Lecturer in Sociology at Goldsmiths, University of London, and part of the editorial board of *Historical Materialism*. He is the translator of several works by Alain Badiou and author of *The Theatre of Production* (Palgrave Macmillan, 2006) and *Fanaticism* (Verso, 2010).

Hilary Wainwright is Editor at *Red Pepper*, Research Director of the New Politics programme at the Transnational Institute and Senior Research Associate at the International Centre for Participation Studies, University of Bradford. She is the author of *Arguments for a New Left* (Blackwell, 1994), *Reclaim the State* (Verso, 2003) and *Public Service Reform* (Picnic, 2009).

Introduction
What Are We Struggling For?

Federico Campagna and Emanuele Campiglio

THE DANCE

It might be true that chaos gives birth to dancing stars, but within a late-capitalist system, the chaos produced by global financial crises seems to be giving birth to other, darker, dancing entities.

These are the times of the dance of financiers, sliding between the whirls of virtual credit and the sturdy glass-concrete towers of first-class lives. The hectic times of crumbling nations, crawling on their knees along the dance floor, surrounded by the ghosts of past mistakes and rachitic futures. The thundering times of war-dances between slow workers and hyper-fast production schedules, between rigid gender structures and liquid identities, between fully armed police and fully enraged people. These are the suspended times of the legion of the unemployed, who sit in the corners and wait for the light to come up and reveal their worthlessness, or the worthlessness of the dance. Some might say, most of all, these are the fastening times of the death-dance of the environment, as it gets pushed, pulled, ripped out of balance.

This book appears as a clandestine sound-system, breaking into the chaos of the global dance. It is a collection of syncopated rhythms, short interventions, ideas, remixes, contaminations. The voices contained in this book are just a few of those blossoming day after day in the four corners of the planet. Some of them come from the rooms of the Academy, some from the offices of official think-tanks, some from the squats and the barricades, some from the occupied squares of many a global metropolis. All of them, however, are part of the bundle of currents which constitutes the growing resistance of millions of people against the deadly rhythms of financial capitalism and of State repression.

US

As if stuck within a new Warsaw Ghetto, the multitudes of the early twenty-first century are struggling to organise their resistance. Their front is fragmented, conflicted, unsure about the outcome of the fight. Some of them are committed to pure non-violence, while some push for escalating the level of conflict. Some advocate the necessity of a structured movement, while others propose a free federation of individuals as the best strategic choice. Some seek compromise with their enemies, some pose the struggle as a matter of victory or death. Some call themselves 'the 99%', others question the very possibility of a collective identity.

Indeed, who are they? Who are we, as we prepare the ammunition and supplies for an all-out resistance? During much of the twentieth century, the answer would have come easily: we are the proletariat, fighting against the bonds of capital. In the early 2000s, the era of the 'movement of the movements' and of the alter-globalisation experience, this answer would have become a little more vague: we are the insurgent multitudes, rebelling against the rule of global capitalism. Today, in a time in which 'there is a war machine in every niche' – to borrow Deleuze and Guattari's definition of fascism – this answer becomes even more difficult.

As will become clear from the very pluralist composition of this collection of texts, 'us' is not a unitarian concept. If we are to embrace the concept of a social body, we must accept the fragmented character of this body and of its mind – or general intellect – as a constitutive element of its nature. To use Deleuze's parlance, the social body does not constitute an abstract, social 'individual', but rather a 'dividual', which is constitutively split, ruptured, dispersed, interrupted.

This fragmentation can be considered from myriad points of view. Under a numerical lens, we can observe today's exploited and insurgent people as composed of a multitude of singular agents. They are – we are – single persons. It is an interesting word, 'person'. The Latin etymology derives from actors wearing large, wooden masks in the theatre during performances, through which their voice would resonate (*per-sonar*, to sound through). A very revealing etymology, perfectly adapted to the current situation. As opposed to the citizen, constituted as such by its belonging to the city (*cives*), the person is the human who speaks up for him or herself on a public stage. The position of the person is a deeply complex one, which embodies the contradictions of a political act of rebellion performed within a 'spectacular' context. The uprising (in Italian, *la sollevazione*, the 'standing-up' which Franco Berardi Bifo interprets as the ground zero of political action) is thus a moment of brave and solitary contrast against the silent background of the stage, of which the masks of the actors would simply be a scenographic function were it not for their autonomous speaking. We have repeatedly witnessed this contradiction, since the dawn of the mass-media era, through the bitter victory of Situationism and up until the world-televised uprisings of the so-called Arab Spring. Politics of rebellion seem increasingly to incorporate the struggle between the voice and the limiting conditions in which it can be heard, between resistance and the annihilating counter-revolution of its spectacle.

It is perhaps only to dust off this loneliness that these voices have a tendency to look for each other. Most often, their encounter happens under coercive circumstances, as is the case with co-workers, inmates and temporary communities of migrants. However, since the triumph of global neoliberalism and the expansion of its productive system into every aspect of life, such a coercive environment is no longer to be found only in designated areas, but becomes a default element of contemporary existence. In the global prison of bio-production, possibilities of encounter between voices are everywhere. As the desire to congregate originates from anguish and desperation – as Camus beautifully noted in several passages of *The Plague* – contemporary society offers plenty of opportunities for that desire to arise.

These new social formations – the struggling 'us' – do not come to life as the rational, conscious organisation of 'Historical forces', as was the case with most movements of the twentieth century, but they find their *raison d'être* in the interplay of the negative emotion of anguish and the positive desire of rebellion. The tendency to create multiplying communities of struggle has thus to be understood as the direct practice of an affective necessity, rather than as the implementation of a pre-existing, strategic vision. Even the general intellect has an unconscious, and many of the current behaviours of the rebellious social body have to be located there. In particular, the creation of new networks of resistance, springing up everywhere in today's world, and emerging as a public phenomenon in the wave of occupations that has taken over countless spaces in cities like Cairo, New York, London, Madrid, Rome and so on.

RESISTANCE

The fact that political will follows – instead of founding – the decision of joining forces, does not mean that politics has exited the scene of resistance. On the contrary, political and strategic thinking are of the utmost importance for the success of the current global, 'dividual' movement. Simply put, it is no longer a politics of flags, but one of direct action. As far back as 1845, Max Stirner already put into words the feeling that animates today's struggle: 'What matters the party to me? I shall find enough anyhow who unite with me without swearing allegiance to my flag.' What we are facing, then, is a movement that attempts to escape the traps of identity, in favour of an approach based on practice. It is because of this new approach that, without having to state it, forces from all colours of the left-wing spectrum have recently managed to converge on shared objectives: from the anarchists to the social democrats, from the communists to the environmental activists, from the autonomists to the reformists, and so on.

Within this movement, prefigurative politics go hand in hand with the desire for long-term, broad-horizon imagination.

Indeed, these two approaches feed into each other. Direct action, understood as prefigurative politics, is at the same time the putting-into-practice of precedent imaginations, and the continuous exercise of testing the imaginary landscapes against the necessities and the subterranean flows of daily life. It is not a coincidence that some of the most interesting experiences of struggle have recently emerged from the world of students and professionals of the education system. Under these circumstances, struggle becomes a moment of self-education, as well as of endless cultural production.

Consequently, the role of intellectuals – one of the most stable and conservative categories inherited from the twentieth century – is now undergoing a process of deep transformation. Following Gramsci's intuition, the role of intellectuals is shifting from its more traditional aspects towards the work of organisation. In a framework of struggle mostly based on direct action, and in a world in which capitalism has developed into an all-pervasive semio-capitalism, the production of culture evolves into the organisation of those spaces, times, structures, and incomes which make the production of autonomous and emancipatory bio-culture possible. Clearly, within a movement grounded on ideas of autonomy and self-organisation, such organisational tasks are no longer the duty of a small number of specialists. Today's resistance makes the concept of management explode, and replaces it with an infinite trust in the capabilities of singular and collective bodies to administer themselves.

However, the organisational element has not monopolised the whole spectrum of intellectual activity. Another crucial aspect of the work of intellectuals remains at the forefront of the struggle. It is the more solitary, inward side of the labour of imagination: the ability to travel through, and simultaneously to construct, possible alternative landscapes for social composition. It is the activity of the pioneers, who describe the world that they have built through their chanting, like the Aborigines along the Song Lines, more than that of the prophet, announcing a fateful destiny for the world. This activity of giving voice to the eyes is the tireless rhapsody which naturally flows out of those fragments of life subtracted from the rule of servitude and exploitation. It is the result of what Cicero denominated 'the dignified rest' (*otium cum dignitate*), the culture which emerges from a state of freedom. It is intellectual activity at its purest, that is, as the simple by-product of a liberated fragment of life.

   They used to call it utopian thinking, when the world still had the reassuring appearance of an island of reality floating in the dangerous waters of 'non-places'. Today, in a time of explicit *mestizaje* between virtuality and reality, the distinction between *topoi* (places) and *u-topoi* (non-places) no longer holds. In the terminal age of what Mark Fisher calls *Capitalist Realism*, we can all witness the foundations of the current reality system dissolving, unveiling the starkly u-topian nature of the system we live in. U-topia, in its most pejorative sense, is already the name of a world which has been turned into thin air by the ethereal fantasy of financial capitalism and semio-capitalism. A world which cannot advocate for itself any plausible status of reality, apart from that imposed with the violence of war. Today, a thought which desires to move beyond itself has to face the journey into the unknown without the reassuring distinction between what is and what is not. Today more than ever, to see is to create, and to create is to make visible. And the routes of this journey are no longer those of armchair pondering, but the steep arteries of adventure. We might call this travelling thought 'emancipatory cartography'. And that is what this book is about.

THIS BOOK

This book originates from a conference organised by Federico Campagna and Emanuele Campiglio at the Institute for Contemporary Arts, London, on 19 March 2011. The conference was scheduled exactly one week before the national day of strikes and direct action of 26 March and was aimed at bringing together a plurality of radical voices to discuss the positive aspects of the struggle. That is, what the then emerging struggle was for, rather than against.

   Several of the contributors to this volume spoke at the conference, namely (in alphabetical order), Milford Bateman,

Franco Berardi 'Bifo', Mark Fisher, David Graeber, Peter Hallward, John Holloway, Saul Newman, Ann Pettifor, Richard Seymour, Andrew Simms, and Hilary Wainwright.

Shortly after the conference, several of the speakers and the organisers discussed the possibility of developing the theme of the event into a more permanent, volume form. In their opinion, the production of a book would overcome the geographical distances and time constraints which necessarily limit the breadth of a physical event.

Other writers were invited to join the temporary think-tank built around the conference: Michael Albert, Shaun Chamberlin, Zillah Eisenstein, Owen Jones, Dan Hind, Christian Marazzi, Nina Power, Marina Sitrin, Mark J. Smith, South London Solidarity Federation, and Alberto Toscano. And of course, Pluto Press was the ideal candidate to be the publisher for a project such as this.

As will be clear from a quick look at the list of contributors, plurality was a concept at the core both of the organisation of the conference and of the production of this volume. While never intended as an absolute value, plurality was seen in both cases as a viable political strategy, through which it was possible to federate similar (yet singular) political positions, rather than forcing them under one party banner. The idea of a temporary federation of forces, organised around a set of issues and demands, was already in the air in the spring of 2011, and it later exploded in the winter of that same year with the wave of occupation movements all over the world.

The original idea for this book came from the volume *What Would it Mean to Win?* by the Turbulence Collective.[1] Their daring yet practical approach, their openness and sharpness of vision, have been an invaluable source of inspiration in the conceptualisation of the present volume.

NOTE

1. Turbulence Collective, *What Would it Mean to Win?* (PM Press, 2010).

Part 1
New Economics

This section explores possible, alternative ways of imagining economic practice.

Michael Albert begins with an overview of the shortcomings of capitalism, which he presents through facts and examples. Against the failures of capitalism, Albert proposes and presents in detail the practice of Parecon, or 'participatory economics'.

Ann Pettifor engages with the causes and development of the financial crisis, to which she opposes an alternative way of understanding and dealing with money and finance, paying special attention to environmental issues. At the core of her analysis is the belief that 'power is not revealed by striking hard or often, but by striking true'.

Milford Bateman focuses on the myths of microfinance and the risks involved in spreading the neoliberal paradigm to local communities, especially in the Global South. Drawing on examples from Italy, the Basque Countries and Vietnam, Bateman shows how it is already possible to imagine and to practise new, cooperative and community-owned forms of financial and economic organisation.

Shaun Chamberlin addresses the relationship between struggles and their 'stories', while exploring the economic practices of the Transition movement and the Tradable Energy Quotas. Through these examples, Chamberlin draws out the story of our relationship with the 'Lover Earth', and the creation of a new meaning which 'makes hope possible'.

1

Participatory Economics from Capitalism

Michael Albert

In the words of the great British economist John Maynard Keynes: '[Capitalism] is not a success. It is not intelligent, it is not beautiful, it is not just, it is not virtuous – and it doesn't deliver the goods. In short, we dislike it, and we are beginning to despise it. But when we wonder what to put in its place, we are extremely perplexed.'[1] Let's see if we can undo some of the perplexity. First, what's the real problem with capitalism?...

Capitalism is theft. The harsh and subservient labours of most citizens fantastically enrich an elite who, if they so choose, don't have to labour at all. On the upper West Side of New York City, within a mile of one another, there exist neighbourhoods in which the average disposable income is, on the poorer side, about $5,000 per year, and, on the richer side, about $500,000 per year. The richest people in the US have wealth unparalleled in history. The poorest people in the US live under bridges inside threadbare cardboard shelters, or they stop living at all. This gap is not explained by a difference in industriousness, in talent, etc. It is a social product, a theft, and the gap between rich and poor nations, as we all know, is even more dramatic.

Capitalism is alienation and anti-sociality. Within capitalism the motives guiding decisions are pecuniary not personal, selfish not social. We each seek individual advance at the expense of others. The result, unsurprisingly, is an anti-social environment in which nice guys finish last. Benefits for the weak arise only as a by-product, not as intended, and often not at all. As but one example, in American hospitals a few hundred thousand people a year die of diseases they did not have when they entered. This is in considerable part a matter of hygiene and other correctable problems. There is no massive campaign to save those lives. It would not be profitable. What health we attain, we attain because someone was seeking not health, but profit. Health, humanity, is impoverished even as profits soar.

Capitalism is authoritarian. Within its workplaces those who labour at rote and tedious jobs have virtually zero say over the conditions, output, and purpose of their efforts. Those who own or who monopolise empowering positions have the preponderant say, in some cases more so even than dictators. Corporations bear as much resemblance to democracy as killing fields do to peace.

Capitalism is inefficient. Market profit-seeking squanders the productive capacities of about 80 per cent of the population by training them primarily to endure boredom and to take orders, not to fulfil their greatest potentials. It wastes inordinate resources on producing sales that aren't beneficial, and on enforcing work assignments that are coerced and therefore resisted.

Capitalism is racist and sexist. This is not intrinsic to the relations of production, but occurs because under the pressure of market competition owners will inevitably exploit racial and gender hierarchies produced in other parts of society. If extra-economic factors reduce the bargaining power of some actors while raising that of others and impact expectations about who should rule and who should obey, capitalists will take note.

Capitalism is violent. The race for capitalist market domination produces nations at odds with other nations until those who accrue sufficient offensive might exploit the resources and populations of those lacking defensive means, including unleashing unholy war.

Capitalism is unsustainable. The money grabbers accumulate and accumulate, regardless of human need and desire, and ignoring or wilfully obscuring the impact not only on workers and consumers, but also on today's environment and tomorrow's resources.

The market propels short-term calculations and makes dumping waste on others to avoid costs an easy and unavoidable avenue to gain. The results are visible in sky and soil, mitigated, as with other capitalist induced suffering, only by social movements that force wiser behaviour.

For at least a decade, only a relatively few people have been made so immoral by their advantages, or so profoundly ignorant by their advanced educations, or so manipulated by media and their own naiveté, that they fail to see that capitalism is a gigantic holocaust of injustice and suffering, and that, as Keynes says, is neither intelligent, nor beautiful, nor just, nor virtuous – and is not even delivering the goods.

So what do we want instead?

Participatory Economics (*parecon*), the replacement for capitalism that I advocate, is built on four institutional commitments.

First, the broad structures by which people participate in economic life and decision-making are nested workers' and consumers' councils of the sort we have seen arise throughout history. The added feature of *parecon*'s councils is a commitment to self-management as the logic of decision-making. People should influence decisions relative to how they are in turn affected by them.

Sometimes self-management could require one-person one-vote and majority rule. Sometimes it could require that a different tally is needed, or that only some segment of the whole populace votes, or that for those who are deciding consensus is needed. All such options are tactics to attain the appropriate degree of self-management for all involved actors.

Second, remuneration in a *parecon* is in accord with effort and sacrifice, not with the output either of one's property or of one's labours, and not with bargaining power either. Other things being equal, in a *parecon* we will earn more if we work longer, if we work harder, or if we work under more harsh or harmful conditions. Remuneration is for duration, intensity, and harshness endured – and not for property, power, or output.

Parecon rejects the idea that someone should earn by virtue of having a deed in his or her pocket. There is no moral warrant for that, nor is there any incentive warrant for it. It also rejects a thuggish economy in which one gets what one can take, as in market exchange. And, most controversially, *parecon* rejects the idea that we should get back from the economy the amount we contributed to it by our personal labours. *Parecon* understands that our output depends on many factors we can't control: having better tools, or working in a more productive environment, or producing more valued items, or having innate qualities that increase our productivity. Economic incentives need to induce productive labour even when it is onerous. *Parecon*'s remuneration scheme makes both moral and economic sense.

Third, participatory economics needs a new division of labour. If a new economy were to remove private profit and incorporate self-managing councils with remuneration for effort and sacrifice, but were to simultaneously retain the current corporate division of labour, its commitments would be inconsistent.

Having 20 per cent of the workforce monopolise largely empowering and more pleasurable work and leaving 80 per cent left with more rote, stultifying, and less pleasurable work, as is the case with the corporate division of labour, guarantees that the former group – I want to call them the coordinator class – will rule over the latter group, or the working class.

Even with a formal commitment to self-management, the coordinators, by virtue of the work they do, will enter each decision-discussion having set the agenda for it, owning the information relevant to debate, possessing the habits of communication that will inform it, and exuding the confidence and energy to fully participate. The workers, in contrast, having been deadened and exhausted by the work they do, will come to decision-discussions only disempowered and exhausted. The coordinators will therefore determine outcomes. In time they will choose to remunerate themselves more, to streamline meetings and decision-making processes by excluding those below, and to orient economic decisions in their own ruling class interests.

One kind of class that exists above workers is the owning class, as we all know. By virtue of a deed, owners in capitalism dispose over the means of production, including hiring and firing wage slaves. But even with this class division eliminated, classlessness is not necessarily attained. Another group that is also defined by its position in the economy, albeit differently, can wield virtually complete power and aggrandise itself above workers. To avoid this coordinator class rule requires that we replace the familiar corporate division of labour with a new approach to defining work roles.

This third institutional commitment of *parecon* requires what we call balanced job complexes. Each of us who works at some job, in any society, good or bad, will by definition be doing some collection of tasks. If the economy employs a corporate division of labour our tasks will combine into a job that is either largely empowering or largely disempowering. In a participatory economy, by contrast, we combine tasks into jobs so that for each person the overall empowerment effect of their job is like the overall empowerment effect of every other person's job. Everyone has an average balanced job complex.

We don't have managers and assemblers, editors and secretaries, surgeons and nurses. The functions these actors now fulfil persist in a *parecon*, but the labour is divided up differently. Of course some people do surgery while most don't, but those who take scalpel to brains also clean bed pans, or sweep floors, or assist with other hospital functions. The total empowerment the surgeon's job affords is altered by remixing tasks. She now has a balanced job complex conveying the same total empowerment and pleasure as the new job of the person who previously only cleaned up.

The domination of what I call the coordinator class over all other workers is removed not by eliminating empowering tasks, or by everyone doing the same things, both of which are not only irrational but impossible – nor by just extolling rote work as important, which is possible and even familiar historically, but which is structurally vacuous – but by distributing both empowering and rote work so that all economic actors are able to participate in self-managed decision-making without advantage or disadvantage due to their economic roles.

Finally, fourth, participatory economics also opts for a new approach to allocation. Instead of markets or central planning, it utilises what it calls participatory planning. The workers' and consumers' councils cooperatively negotiate inputs and outputs in light of the full social and ecological costs and benefits and with actors having a self-managing say. (A full discussion of this allocation system, and of the other key features of *parecon*, is available in many books and essays, including online.)

The claim we make for combining workers and consumers' councils, self-managed decision-making, remuneration for effort and sacrifice, balanced job complexes, and participatory planning, is not only that the system is classless and promotes values that we hold dear, such as solidarity, diversity and equity, but also that, to the extent possible and with no recurring biases, it apportions to each worker and consumer an appropriate level of self-managing influence in relation to each economic decision. More, it offers a minimalist list of institutional features designed to achieve these ends. It is not a blueprint, and does not overreach itself, but instead takes simple well-tested insights to their logical conclusions.

Parecon doesn't reduce productivity but rather provides adequate and proper incentives to work. It has no bias towards longer hours but allows for a free choice of work versus leisure. It doesn't pursue what is most profitable regardless of the impact on workers, on the environment, and often even on consumers, but reorients output towards what is truly beneficial in light of the full social and environmental costs and benefits and of people's freely developed self-managed preferences.

Parecon doesn't waste the human talents of the people now doing surgery, or composing music, or otherwise engaging in difficult and skilled labour, by requiring that they undertake less empowering labour as well; rather, by way of this requirement, there surfaces a gargantuan reservoir of previously untapped talents throughout the populace while empowering and rote labour is apportioned not only justly, but in accord with true and full self-management and classlessness.

Parecon doesn't assume sociable much less divine citizens. Rather it creates an institutional context in which, in order to get ahead in their economic engagements, even people who grow up entirely self-seeking and anti-social must be concerned for the general social good and the well being of others.

Finally, what difference does advocating *parecon* – once one has a full and informed view of it – make for our behaviour in the present?

When Margaret Thatcher said 'There is no alternative', she accurately identified a central obstacle to masses of people actively seeking a better world. If one sincerely believes there is no better future, then rejecting a call to fight against poverty, alienation, and even war is understandable. Indeed, for those who sincerely think capitalism is here to stay, to fight against it, or even against its symptoms, can seem like a fool's errand.

Advocates of *parecon* seek to provide a vision that will turn that feeling upside-down, replacing cynicism with hope and reason. When we go to movies and see courageous souls of the past represented on the screen, fighting against slavery, or against the subordination of women, or against colonialism, or for peace and justice and against dictatorships, we rightly feel sympathy and admiration for these acts. The abolitionists, the suffragettes, the labour union organisers, the anti-Apartheid activists, those overthrowing dictators, all the seekers of freedom and dignity are heroes for us.

But if we admire their standing up against injustice, we ought ourselves to stand up against injustice. If we admire their seeking a better world, we should ourselves seek a better world. If we admire their rejection of exploitation, alienation, domination, and its violent maintenance, we should ourselves advocate and fight for an economic model and societal structure that will eliminate these horrors – and I would argue that participatory economics offers such a model and should be part of such a new society.

NOTE

1. John Maynard Keynes, "National Self-Sufficiency", *The Yale Review* 22:4 (June 1933), Section 3.

2

Let Ideas and Art be International, Goods be Homespun, and Finance Primarily National

Ann Pettifor

Power is not revealed by striking hard or often, but by striking true.

Honoré de Balzac

I want to start on a positive note. As the 'Arab Spring' of 2011 demonstrated, transformations can happen – and can happen quite suddenly. Things can 'flip' in a startlingly short time. A social movement can build, mobilise and bring about great changes. However, meaningful change cannot happen unless we – i.e. civil society – fully understand the causes of oppression; the means for ending structural imbalances in power relationships, and why a transformation is needed. Unless, that is, we strike true.

We are faced by a quadruple crunch: the climate crunch, the energy crunch, and the credit crunch – the last of which has led to global financial crisis and an 'unemployment crunch'. We have to deal with these crises, but to do so we need a monetary system, a financial system, that serves both society's needs and the needs of the ecosystem.

Geoffrey Ingham explains the problem well: 'money is not only "infrastructural" power, it is also "despotic" power. In other words, money expands human society's capacity to get things done, but this power can be appropriated by particular interests ... The production of money is ... a source of power.'[1]

In my experience, very few people – including mainstream economists, but also environmentalists and eco-warriors – understand the financial system, or the nature of credit, a cornerstone of all modern money, banking systems and economies. At a personal level we in the west, as individuals, have a conflicted relationship with money – it is both mundane and mysterious to us. We use it every day, routinely, rarely leaving the house without cash or our credit card. Simultaneously we are in awe of money, mystified by it, and fearful of its power over us. Many prefer to be in denial about its true nature and origins. And those who have the greatest power over money – central bankers and private bankers – deny society the transparency and accountability that would lead to a proper understanding of the nature of credit and money, and of the role of the banking system in creating and distributing that credit.

Few of us understand, for example, that savings are not necessary prior to investment. That the money for a loan is not in the bank until the borrower applies for the loan, and provides collateral and a promise to repay. That credit – created out of thin air – can finance investment. That credit creates, first, economic activity (jobs, projects, works), then income, and finally, savings. Not the other way around. In other words, we do not need savings in order to invest. Banks do not need deposits in order to create credit. Credit – which can be created by a keystroke on a computer – creates economic activity, and what follows from that activity are the deposits, income and savings that result.

All of this should be common knowledge. It was certainly known to, for example, John Law in the seventeenth century;[2] to President Lincoln in the nineteenth century; to President Roosevelt, John Maynard Keynes,[3] John Kenneth Galbraith[4] and Joseph Schumpeter in the twentieth century. Despite their great contributions to our understanding of the credit system, the 'science' of credit and money is mostly discussed and deliberated in language that is arcane, designed to obscure from public understanding the true nature of the workings of the financial system.

But then in 2008 things changed. The central bankers of the EU, the United States and Japan raised, in full public view, an extraordinary and almost unimaginable sum of money: $14 trillion.[5] This was raised in one year to bail out bankrupt private financial institutions. The phrase 'quantitative easing' broke through and entered public discourse.

Although the language is new to the public, the process is not. In fact central banks had been conjuring credit 'out of thin air' both before and since 1694 – when the venerable Bank of England was established. To verify that credit is created in this way, on 16 March 2009, Ben Bernanke, the governor of the Federal Reserve, gave the first-ever interview by a Fed governor to the CBS *60 Minutes*[6] show. It was the day after the Fed had bailed out AIG for the sum of $160 billion.

Bernanke was asked by the journalist on CBS's show: 'Where did you raise that money from? Was it tax money?' He replied: 'No, it's not tax money. The banks have accounts with the Fed, much the same way that you have an account in a commercial bank. So, to lend to a bank, we simply use the computer to mark up the size of the account that they have with the Fed.'

So with just a few key strokes, $160 billion was created for the benefit of AIG. And thank heavens it was. The banking system, unlike you or I, can 'magic' money out of nothing – and this, in the case of AIG, prevented, for a while at least, global financial meltdown.

This ability to create credit is one of the achievements of western civilisation. Not all societies have banking systems that can function in this way – in some of the poorest parts of the world people carry around bags of money because they don't trust their banks or their banking system. But in those countries where there is a developed banking system, economic progress can occur. Thanks to a developed banking system, we can, in the words of John Maynard Keynes, 'afford what we can do'. Not more than we can do; and not more than the ecosystem can stand. But we can afford to tackle climate change with a well-developed banking system; we can afford to care for people with Alzheimer's; we can afford to support artists and the creative sector; we can afford beautiful works of art and music, and fine, safe cities and parks.

The enormous and wondrous power of a developed banking system is indeed a public good, one that exists only in societies with sound, carefully regulated forms of governance and strong legal systems. Because banking is dependent on publicly financed infrastructure (a legal and criminal justice system that enforces contracts; well-developed accounting systems, etc.), we taxpayers have a right to hold bankers to account for the effective privatisation of this great power, and for economic stability and well-being.

However, as things stand, and as a result of deregulation and financial liberalisation begun in the UK and the US in 1971, society has little power to regulate and oversee the largely privatised 'market-based' banking system. Nevertheless, banking gains are privatised while bankers demand their losses be nationalised. On our behalf, politicians have, since the 1960s and 1970s, conceded the enormous power of the banking system to create credit to small elites that run the now monopolised and globalised private banks. We continue to accept that because private banks have expanded beyond our borders they are, and should remain, beyond our control.

Until the recent financial meltdown, we turned a blind eye to the activities of those who run private banks: some of the most fraudulent, irresponsible and amoral members of society. Instead we happily turned up at their financial 'party'; grabbed their easy if costly credit cards – and went on wild shopping sprees. Now that we are being disciplined for our borrowing, now that we are more aware of fraud and amorality in banking, we can find no way of penalising and disciplining the lenders – those at the helm of the banks. Instead, as Yves Smith notes, our government and taxpayer-backed central banks have extended an 'extraordinary level of support ... to major banks during the crisis and now, via measures like super low interest rates and continued regulatory forbearance ... continue to maintain the fiction that they are private companies'.[7] Smith asks why, given these levels of subsidy, our central banks do not 'treat (banks) as humble utilities and regulate them accordingly?'

Why indeed.

* * *

To illustrate both the benign and the malign sides of the banking system, we can review recent events in Japan post the March 2011 tsunami. In the face of that catastrophic natural crisis, and the consequent meltdown of a nuclear power station, the Bank of Japan (BoJ) created, almost immediately, about £185 billion by means of that process now known as 'quantitative easing' (QE). The Bank rightly took this action to deal with an urgent, unprecedented and devastating crisis. But while central banks can create credit effortlessly, the burden then falls on the rest of the (private) banking system to ensure that this publicly created finance cascades down through the private banking system to the real economy – providing affordable (i.e. low interest rate) loans to borrowers. This could include government departments and private construction companies that need finance to urgently hire the labour needed to, e.g., undertake reconstruction and restoration in devastated areas of Japan. Their economic activity will then generate returns: in the form of a) income and savings deposited in the private banks; and b) taxes paid directly, and indirectly by people in employment, as revenue to government – and used to repay debts.

But QE does not always flow into productive economic activity. For example, because of the deregulation of global capital flows, the QE, or liquidity, generated by the Fed Reserve after 2009 was not all invested by US bankers in the real, productive economy of the United States. Instead that liquidity was largely used for speculation and private gain across the globe – a freedom much prized by private bankers.

However, footloose global capital flows add to the already exceptional burden faced by poorer countries. Massive capital inflows, generated as a result of QE, inflate the local currency, making exports more expensive and flooding local markets with cheap imports. Or they may be faced by the rising cost of food and energy, brought on, in large part, by financial speculation in commodities. And capital mobility may well inflate yet another global asset price bubble, this time in say, gold or oil or Greek bonds. Only to be followed by yet another catastrophic deflation of that same asset price bubble.

As a result of the adoption of neoliberal policies by successive Anglo-American governments (and their counterparts in other western governments), easy but dear money has been used to lure consumers into reckless spending sprees and debt, with interest and amortisation payments absorbing future earnings. Simultaneously, and as a deliberate result of economic policy, earnings in western economies have fallen, and continue to fall in real terms. This decline in incomes as levels of debt rise, hurts the majority. However these policies do not serve the interests of bankers either, as falling incomes and rising debts makes it hard to extract rising 'rents' (in the form of principal and interest payments) from debtors.

So with one hand, neoliberalism encouraged the private creation of vast mountains of costly debt. With the other, it curtailed the growth in both individual corporate and sovereign income that would have helped pay down debts. The cuts in income for individuals and households are mirrored by cuts in, e.g., taxation income for sovereign governments, and in austerity policies that exacerbate the decline in government revenues while increasing spending on welfare payments.

Hence the Eurozone crisis that, as I write, is intensifying the crisis of 2007–9, is an ongoing global banking crisis.

*   *   *

It is important that we understand current events not as a new outbreak of crisis, but as a continuation of the banking crisis that first came to the public's attention in 2007–9. Despite the dishonest rhetoric of bankers and their political friends, this crisis is not a crisis of government finances. It is not a crisis of sovereign debt and deficits. These are simply the symptoms of a private banking crisis, as governments absorb the losses of private bankers. The crisis of 2007–12, which is ongoing, is first and foremost a private banking crisis. The 'debtonation'[8] of 9 August 2007 occurred when banks lost confidence in the viability of other banks, and stopped lending to each other. After a year when the fuse of huge debts endured a 'slow burn', the 2008 Lehman bankruptcy exploded the financial system and threatened systemic failure.

Without consulting taxpayers, central bankers and politicians rushed to the aid of the bankrupt financiers who were now in charge of a broken banking system. Banks that had been lending machines were transformed into borrowing machines, a bizarre development.

Politicians, many of them in hock to private bankers, provided taxpayer guarantees, and socialised private losses by transferring these on to the shoulders of taxpayers. Central bankers pushed interest rates down to very low levels, to provide further support to bankers. Thanks to the weakness of politicians of both left and right, as well as the impotence of central bankers, this nation-alisation of private losses was offered almost unconditionally to an immensely wealthy, arrogant and stupid elite. No attempt was made to re-structure the banks, to regulate their activities effectively, and so restore global financial stability.

While politicians, central bankers and economists in the UK and US applied only weak stimulus measures to the real economy, and did little to ameliorate a) the high levels, and rapidly de-leveraged levels, of debt, and b) the falling incomes and profits of individuals and entrepreneurs, they continued to give valuable taxpayer-backed support to the private finance sector. By 2010, private debts in the UK were 469 per cent of GDP and rising.[9]

Financial liberalisation has failed, catastrophically.

By the end of 2011 policies for 'austerity' were adopted across most western economies. They marked the final failure of the existing arrangement between public interests and the interests of private wealth. The banking system has bitten the governmental hand that feeds it, and now increasingly threatens the world with collapse, global economic depression, social degradation and political upheaval.

The only way forward is a new arrangement, based on ones that have better served societies since the dawn of civilisation. The only genuine solution to the crisis must involve a large-scale reversal of liberalisation.

*   *   *

The Euro may only be one aspect of the liberalised architecture, but it is a major component and a pernicious one. Thanks to the failed orthodoxy of liberal finance, sovereign countries that joined the Euro have been denied the benefits of a monetary system enjoyed by, e.g., the UK and the US. The central banks of sovereigns like Greece and Portugal are forbidden from creating credit, in the form of, e.g., QE. The ECB, which is responsible for the Eurozone as a whole, and for the EU's foreign reserves, is forbidden by EU treaties (see Article 125 of the Treaty on European Union[10]) from providing finance to the governments of the Eurozone. Instead, sovereign governments like Greece and Ireland can only borrow from private banks, freed by 'the invisible hand' to lend to sovereign governments at very high, real rates.

These sovereign, supposedly democratic governments have no control over the rate of interest appropriate to their economy; nor do they have a currency over which they can exercise some control. And yet they remain accountable to their people for the national security of their country.

The Euro is the antithesis of a democratic currency, which should be deployed to support a nation's economic activity. The currency and the banking system should be there to support the weak and restrain the strong. Instead the Euro benefits the strong at the expense of the weak; the private at the expense of the public. As such it can play no part in monetary reform, and must therefore be dismantled.

The Euro must be understood not as a currency of the peoples, but as an ideal of private wealth. It is a currency which detaches the credit-creation system from democratic oversight and delegates those immense powers to private, unaccountable bankers – to use for private gain.

For the Euro is a perversion of the greatest monies in history. These arose as a relation between people and the state. Through the institutional development of central banks, domestic banks, state borrowing, paper currency and double-entry book keeping, national monies have underpinned all of the economic development of the greatest societies of the world.

Money, when used most effectively, has been aimed at the interests of society, of productive labour, and vibrant state and private activity alike. But the Euro is a money or currency aimed only at the interests of private wealth. It is divorced from individual nation states.

If the Eurozone countries were to regain policy autonomy, to restore and rebuild their own central banks, then their currencies, their monetary system, and their social, private and financial interests could be re-aligned. Prosperity could be reignited. Issued through the central bank and domestic retail banks, a nation's currency can help finance and underpin a programme of public works expenditures, and in parallel, through multiplier processes, the spending of newly earned income to revive private activity.

Of course a central bank has to carefully regulate the creation of credit: the creation of too much credit than there is economic potential within a country will lead to inflation. Conversely, the creation of too little credit – as is happening now – will lead to a deflationary spiral. But these are matters best judged by central bankers and their expert staff – answerable to democratic institutions. If left to the 'invisible hand of the market', that is, the private interests of wealth, the inflation of excess credit for speculation, greed and private gain will be the inevitable result, as the last three inflationary decades have proved.

Jobs, economic activity and prosperity – within the limits of the ecosystem – can be restored. The expertise to facilitate such a transition exists. It has been done before – successfully. The last time the world threw off the chains of private banking wealth was in the 1930s. Then, Britain led the way. In September 1931, financial interests demanded high interest rates and austerity as the impact of the credit crunch and banking crisis of 1929 and the Great Depression hammered the people. At this point Britain, like Greece today, became defiant. The UK threw off its fetters and left the gold standard – the Euro of a century ago.

Under Keynes's tutelage, Sterling replaced the gold standard and was revived as a money managed by the Bank of England and, through capital controls, protected from speculative and vested interest. Then in 1934, President Roosevelt freed the US from 'nine mocking years with the golden calf and three long years of the scourge' (FDR Speech at Madison Square Garden, 31 October 1936). The American economy bailed out of that era's equivalent of the Euro and its so-called 'stability and growth programme'.

President Roosevelt freed the dollar from 'the fetters' of gold, and the American people from the 'scourge' of austerity.

The US government then embarked on the finest programme of public works expenditures known in modern history. Great public buildings were erected, symphony orchestras established, writers were sponsored (not least John Steinbeck), fantastic murals created, swimming pools built. When, in 1935, a socialist government took power in France and freed the Franc from the fetters of the gold standard, only the fascist economies remained in thrall to the gold standard and private wealth.

Interrupted by war, and diluted at Bretton Woods in 1947, finance was still regulated; restrained as servant, not master, through the age of economic and social advance from 1945 to 1970.

Today, the likelihood of the UK or US once again taking this lead – and defending society from the predations of private wealth – is slim indeed. But there is no theoretical reason why the lead should not be taken by a smaller nation – like Greece.

The history of the world teaches us the ebb and flow of prosperity between nations. It would be fitting too if a new era was to arise from the cradle of western civilisation.

My passionate ambition is to ensure that activists in the green movement turn their attention for a moment from environmental issues and focus instead on the financial system, and the role it plays in fuelling credit-creation, consumption and, with rising consumption, rising emissions.

The fundamental fact is this: there is a direct link between 'easy money', 'eBay shopping' and 'easyJet': between easy money, consumption and rising toxic emissions. If we don't turn our attention to reclaiming democratic oversight and regulation of the financial system, we are not going to able to transform and de-carbonise our economy.

If we don't understand the links between easy money at very high rates of return and the rate of exploitation of the ecosystem, and if we don't see how these are all tied in together, we are never going to be able to address the impending threat of climate change. Because: 'power is not revealed by striking hard or often, but by striking true'.

NOTES

1. Geoffrey Ingham, *The Nature of Money* (Polity Press, 2004).
2. John Law urged the establishment of a national bank to create and increase instruments of credit in a text entitled *Money and Trade Consider'd with a Proposal for Supplying the Nation with Money* (1705), see http://en.wikipedia.org/wiki/John_Law_(economist)
3. John Maynard Keynes, *The General Theory of Employment, Interest, and Money* (Prometheus Books, 1936).
4. John Kenneth Galbraith, *Money: Whence It Came, Where It Went* (Houghton Mifflin, 1975).
5. Andrew G. Haldane, Executive Director, Financial Stability, Bank of England, 'Rethinking the Financial Network', Speech delivered at the Financial Student Association, Amsterdam, April 2009, www.bankofengland.co.uk/publications/speeches/2009/speech409.pdf
6. Ben Bernanke in an interview with CBS News, 16 March 2009, http://www.cbsnews.com/video/watch/?id=4868163n&tag=mncol;lst;8
7. Yves Smith, *Naked Capitalism* blog, 26 April 2011, http://www.nakedcapitalism.com/2011/04/crowdsourcing-questions-for-the-first-press-conference-by-a-fed-chairmantomorrow.html
8. See my blog, www.debtonation.org
9. McKinsey Global Institute, 'Debt and Deleveraging: The Global Credit Bubble and its Economic Consequences', January 2010, p. 18. 'Borrowing accelerated in most developed countries'; 'The United Kingdom experienced the largest increase in total debt relative to GDP from 2000 through 2008 with its ratio reaching 469%', http://www.mckinsey.com/~/media/McKinsey/dotcom/Insights%20and%20pubs/MGI/Research/Financial%20Markets/Debt%20and%20deleveraging%20Global%20credit%20bubble/MGI_Debt_and_deleveraging_full_report.ashx
10. Article 125, Treaty on European Union (as amended by the Treaty of Lisbon 2007), pp. 98–9, http://www.eudemocrats.org/fileadmin/user_upload/Documents/D-Reader_friendly_latest version.pdf

3

A New Local Financial System for Sustainable Communities

Milford Bateman

There is an emerging consensus that, since the 1970s, national and local neoliberal policies have undermined and destroyed far many more communities around the world than have been helped to sustainably and equitably develop and escape poverty. It was not supposed to be this way: free markets, the profit motive and minimal state intervention were long mooted to be the economic and social saviours of humankind.[1] The rise of market fundamentalism in the 1970s, accelerated greatly in the 1980s by the coming to power of Margaret Thatcher in the UK and Ronald Reagan in the US, was expected by its adherents to quickly lead on to major economic and social progress. However, if one leaves out steadily growing China, which initially experimented with neoliberal policies but then quickly backtracked on almost all of them,[2] then compared to the previous quarter century period of Keynesianism and supposedly 'inefficient' forms of state economic management and intervention (1945–70), the outcome of the neoliberal policy model in this latest era has been truly abysmal almost everywhere.[3]

As Minsky long predicted, neoliberal policies were always likely to be especially destructive when played out through the financial sector.[4] From the 1970s onwards, deregulation, privatisation, demutualisation and other similar imperatives associated with neoliberalism were imposed upon *local* financial institutions and systems around the world. The result was chaos and destruction. Local financial institutions established thanks to the heroic efforts and sacrifices of successive generations, such as building societies, financial cooperatives, credit unions and cooperative savings banks, were plunged into a new world of brute market forces, speculation, egregious risk-taking, insider dealing, a 'greed is good' philosophy, and increasingly stratospheric financial rewards paid out to senior managers. Inevitably, large numbers of local financial institutions were progressively looted 'from the inside' and ultimately destroyed. This also helped to seriously undermine and distort the economic and social fabric of the communities in which such local financial institutions were initially established and had operated perfectly well for so many years.

One of the most devastating – and perhaps surprising to some – financial sector failures in recent years is the supposedly progressive concept of microfinance (also known as microcredit). While initially lauded by neoliberals as the ultimate solution to poverty and underdevelopment, no more so than by the Bangladeshi economist and 2006 Nobel Peace Prize winner, Muhammad Yunus,[5] after 30 years of the microfinance movement even long-time supporters now accept that there is no evidence whatsoever to show that the massive international donor community, government and commercial investments into microfinance have had an overall positive impact.[6] Even worse, the microfinance industry and developing countries have increasingly been rocked by a growing number of hugely damaging over-supply-driven 'microfinance meltdowns', notably in Bolivia in 1999, in Morocco and Nicaragua in 2008, in Bosnia starting in 2009, and the very latest, and possibly most destructive to date, in Andhra Pradesh state in India starting in late 2010. It has also not helped the case for microfinance that several of the very largest microfinance institutions that emerged in the 2000s, most notably SKS in India and Compartamos in Mexico, exceeded many Wall Street financial institutions in the way that senior managers were able to effectively 'loot' their own institution via stratospherically high salaries, bonuses, dividends, interest free loans, and, of course, the windfall proceeds from the inevitable Initial Public Offering (IPO).

Compounding the local problems created by microfinance is the diversion of a country's scarce funds (savings, remittances, etc.) away from the most productive local use and into the least productive, if not outright damaging, uses. This is the 'opportunity cost' argument, meaning that more effective alternatives have had to be foregone because funds have been channelled into microfinance applications. All the indications are that microfinance institutions have wastefully absorbed scarce financial resources that would have been better channelled into more sustainable local economic development applications, such as small and medium enterprises (SMEs) and cooperative enterprises.[7]

THE NEED FOR PRO-ACTIVE COMMUNITY-OWNED AND CONTROL FINANCIAL INSTITUTIONS

All told, neoliberal policymakers in governments and the international development community (especially, it must be said, in the Washington DC-based institutions) have inflicted quite catastrophic damage upon long-standing local financial institutions everywhere. Naturally, this is to be greatly regretted. However, the question now is, What sort of local financial institutions do we now need to establish in order to best promote sustainable and equitable local economic and social development?

The first requirement for local financial institutions here is that they be *pro-active* rather more than simply market-conforming. Pro-activity is vital in order to build new local competitive advantages wherever possible, instead of simply allowing historical specialism (in, say, heavy industries) to trap a community in permanent poverty. Communities should not always abide by market rules, since all too often this means they are condemned to 'specialise in poverty', as the saying goes. Instead, even at the local level, there is always the opportunity to 'guide the market'[8] in order to try to develop new local growth trajectories based on careful longer-term investment and by tapping more creatively into sustainable local market (private and public) demand.

One other absolutely core factor that comes across from the recent policy responses to the Great Recession – and it is a trajectory that is very firmly supported by the mass of historical evidence – is that a local financial institution should ideally be owned and controlled by the community in which it operates. There are a number of reasons for this.

First, local community ownership and control will help to ensure that a productive 'local savings and investment cycle' can become the new norm. This cycle has a number of obvious advantages. Local financial institutions know and understand the locality. They also often have a professional/family interest in securing local economic success through careful investments. In practical terms, enterprises with the most potential for sustainable growth, job creation, exporting, solidarity-building, and other positive attributes, can be identified and then carefully nurtured into full operation. Meanwhile on the savings side, local savings mobilisation is often much easier once it becomes known that the end use is to promote the local economy and provide local jobs, not to be lodged in offshore bank accounts, to jack up management salaries to new heights, or used for speculative purposes. All told, as we will see now, the most successful localities stand out as those that have succeeded to build just such 'local savings and investment cycles'. With reference to northern Italy's famously efficient, honest and developmental local banks, Becattini codified this specific local advantage as 'The Theory of the Local Bank'.[9]

Of course, not all such enterprise projects ultimately succeed with local financial support. This is quite normal, as any venture capital operation will tell you. But the experience of many countries and regions overwhelmingly shows that it is perfectly possible to learn how to identify and creatively support *enough* growth-oriented enterprises to make the exercise more than worthwhile. That is, the eventual payback arising from those enterprises that succeed (taxes, new jobs, investments, local subcontracting opportunities, etc.) covers most, if not all, of the upfront costs of the financial and technical support that actually helped bring them to life. The most important point is that the surviving enterprises will constitute the anchor around which the wider local enterprise sector can also begin to develop and ultimately prosper as well.

Another important reason for ensuring local community ownership and control of financial institutions is that otherwise, as the evidence above attests, local financial institutions are very much open to the possibility of being 'captured' by senior employees, and thereafter turned towards fulfilling a purely private enrichment agenda. This possibility is greatly heightened everywhere where the wider business ambience, facilitated by local deregulation, confers sole legitimacy upon the actions of individual entrepreneurs and business-savvy managers. This ambience is, of course, one of the most visible outcomes of neoliberal policies, often termed the 'winner takes all' philosophy.[10] As social anthropologist David Harvey demonstrates, one of the worst impacts of neoliberalism is the way it has given birth to a process of private enrichment through wealth *redistribution*, not wealth *creation*, a process he termed 'accumulation by dispossession'.[11] Here, the process involves managers of local financial institutions 'dispossessing' the community of an institution that might otherwise have promoted community-development goals, but henceforth actually adheres to a revised set of private enrichment goals best achieved by restructuring public and community financial flows and assets into private financial flows and assets.

What is needed here to promote sustainable local economic and social development, then, is clear. We need local financial institutions that are pro-active and where local community ownership and control can help ensure that positive 'local savings and investment cycles' begin to emerge. We also need local institutions wherein negative 'accumulation by dispossession' trajectories can be judiciously avoided as much as possible. Let us go on to consider some of the most important local financial models and community-based financial institutions in order to see exactly how they have been able to promote local development in the way I have described.

GOOD LOCAL EXAMPLES SHOULD HELP SHOW THE WAY FORWARD

A good place to start is to look at the experience of well-designed and managed Community Development Banks. Perhaps the best example is that of the *Caja Laboral Popular* (CLP), the financial arm of the famous Mondragón group of cooperative enterprises that operate in the Basque region of northern Spain. The CLP is a community development bank owned and controlled by the cooperative enterprises in the Basque region attached to the Mondragón group. It is a financial institution that since the 1960s has manifestly succeeded in supporting sustainable cooperative enterprise development in an historically backward and conflict-affected region. Adopting a unique social venture capital mode of operation,[12] the CLP has been able to identify and then support rafts of growth-oriented cooperative enterprises into existence, and then provide ongoing support to allow them to enjoy rapid but sustainable growth and expansion. With a network of more than 120 inter-linked cooperatives, mainly industrial worker cooperatives, and employing more than 80,000 full time member-employees, by the late 2000s the Mondragón group was the most successful cluster of cooperatives in the world.

Compared to the private sector, the wages, benefits and working conditions in the Mondragón cooperatives have always been very good indeed. As cooperatives, there is also the important (albeit, imperfect) element of participation and democratic decision-making, a value that was then projected out into the wider local community. Thanks to its deep roots in the community, and because of various democratic checks and balances, the CLP itself has managed to very successfully steer clear of both corruption and mismanagement. A final indirect benefit enjoyed by the people of Mondragón and wider afield is that the industrial and service cooperatives supported by the CLP also became the lynchpin around which the wider non-cooperative business community was able to develop in a more consensual (or, we might say, less anti-social) way than might otherwise have been the case. For example, with such good conditions enjoyed by those in the CLP-established cooperatives, the private enterprise sector in the wider Basque region found itself having to follow suit in order to attract and retain labour. All told, in a little over 30 years a pro-active set of local financial institutions has helped turn a once poor region into one of

Europe's richest, equality-based, most socially inclusive and culturally vibrant regions.

Broadly similar positive results to Mondragón were achieved in another European region; that of Northern Italy after 1945. This particular experience involved not just one community development bank, but *networks* of cooperative banks, financial cooperatives and local and regional controlled Special Credit Institutes (SCIs). All of these financial institutions were able to work together very well and, at the end of the day, were quite decisive in successfully reconstructing the business and social infrastructure destroyed in the northern regions by the Second World War. By quickly mobilising savings, first of all, and then gradually recycling these savings into long-term investments in potentially sustainable and/or fast growth local businesses, the local economy was quickly able to recover from the War and thereafter to develop and grow very fast. Crucially, very much as in the Basque region, the dominance of cooperative financial institutions naturally encouraged special support for cooperative enterprises in both the industrial and agricultural fields. As Ammirato shows, this helped turn northern Italy into perhaps the world's premier regional location for democratically managed industrial and agricultural enterprises.[13] Perhaps most important of all for those interested in the overall outcome of this local financial model, the region of Emilia Romagna has regularly topped European 'Quality of Life' surveys thanks to the very high levels of solidarity, equality, dignity and sense of 'community liveability' thereby generated. According to Stefano Zamagni of the University of Bologna, 'Social capital is highly associated with quality of life everywhere (and) it seems that the co-operatives' emphasis on fairness and respect contribute to the accumulation of social capital here.'[14]

Spurred on by such uplifting European examples, a growing number of Less Developed Countries (LDCs) have also begun to (re)explore the idea of local cooperative banks and other community-based financial institutions. Indeed, many LDCs now fully accept that the cooperative banking concept is a sound one: the problem is simply one of how to get the governance issues right. Some LDCs have also been spurred on by successes with the development bank concept at the national level in current and former LDCs (e.g., in Brazil). But at the community level, too, there are many creative examples of what can be done when local financial institutions work with development institutions to identify and promote new market sectors. The city of Medellín in Colombia, for example, has pioneered the promotion of equitable local economic and social development outcomes through the local financial sector.[15] Establishing its own social microfinance institution, *Banco de las Opportunidades*, and a pro-active business support body (*Centros de Desarrollo Empresarial Zonal*, CEDEZO is the local acronym), the city government of Medellín has been able to start to develop more sustainable small businesses rather than just the usual raft of unstable 'here today, but gone tomorrow' informal micro-enterprises. Crucially, a good part of the finance required to operate these new pro-poor institutions has come from the city's ownership and good management of the main regional energy company, *Empresas Publicas de Medellín* (EPM), which is mandated to channel 30 per cent of its net annual profit into the city administration's budget.

One valuable aspect of the CEDEZO's operations is that it strongly discourages poor individuals, especially poor women, from entering local market sectors that are manifestly already saturated and, in many cases, demand is already declining. More entry and competition under such circumstances only serves to reduce turnover, volumes, prices and so also profits/ wages for all the market participants. Belatedly entering such an overcrowded market generally means very limited returns for a poor individual, if not almost certain failure. In addition, the new entrants also end up taking valuable market share, and so also income, away from the other equally poor individuals already operating there and struggling to eke out a living. With the CEDEZO's help, however, the poor are encouraged to explore other simple products or services to provide to local customers, or else they are helped to introduce their existing product or service into other local and regional market segments with far more potential (i.e., demand) to ensure business survival and growth. Importantly, the most promising business ideas are increasingly being referred to a range of other free business support servi... providers (technology, business planning, marketing, etc.). This referral service, it is hoped, will help increase the chances of the poor making a success of any slightly more complicated business. The poor are also often advised to rely upon access to a number of local cash grant programmes, partly in order that they hold off until a more sustainable business project comes up. Overall, as Bateman, Duran Ortīz and Sinković conclude,[16] with very high failure rates attached to most microenterprise projects, and so valuable family assets (e.g., land, housing) and other income flows (e.g., remittances, pensions) all too often lost when the poor are forced to repay a microloan attached to a failing microenterprise, it is clearly bad economics (as well as morally reprehensible) to insist that the poor should seek their individual salvation through microenterprise activity, or else simply starve.

Consider, finally, the hugely important 'growth with equity' experiences of the East Asian 'Tiger' economies, which all have an excellent track record of learning from each other and patiently building successful pro-poor local financial systems. As the most recent, and one of the most successful, of these cases, Vietnam's experience has very important implications for other developing countries also seeking to build a local financial system capable of securing local economic and social success. Long one of the poorest countries in South Asia, Vietnam is now very widely seen as having experienced an 'economic miracle' over the last 20 or so years.[17] Poverty has dramatically fallen since 1993 and today the country is nearing middle income status. Crucially, this stunning progress is very much a function of Vietnam's heterodox local financial system, a system that has proved supremely capable of generating rafts of successful growth-oriented SMEs and efficient family farming operations.

The core of Vietnam's local financial model is a mixture of state and community-owned and controlled financial institutions. First, there is the Vietnam Bank for Agriculture and Rural Development (VBARD). The largest bank in Vietnam, VBARD has a network of more than 2,000 branches. VBARD provides ample quantities of credit carefully targeted at microenterprises and small businesses with the potential to quickly and sustainably grow, thereby allowing them to quickly insert themselves into local industrial and agricultural supply chains. Complimenting the activities of VBARD is the Vietnam Bank for Social Policy (VBSP), which focuses upon providing subsidised microcredit to the poor. Interest rates on VBSP loans are even lower than in VBARD, as are the loan sizes. A third complimentary local institution is that of the rafts of People's Credit Funds (PCFs).

Established in 1993 by the State Bank of Vietnam (SBV), the country's central bank, the PCFs are commune-based rural credit institutions based on the *Caisse Populaire* system successfully used in Quebec, Canada. Alongside these three main local financial institutions are a host of other state- and non-state institutions working to provide low-cost (subsidised) credit to the poor as part of local development.

Vietnam's stunning progress since the 1980s is intimately connected to the operation of this unique and interconnected structure of local and community-based state and non-state financial institutions. First of all, the local financial system was responsible for kick-starting a very large number of innovation-driven SMEs. Directly and indirectly (through subcontracting to large companies) it is the new SME sector that effectively lies behind Vietnam's outstanding export performance. Second, Vietnam's family farms were also easily able to tap into very affordable and long-term funds in order to create new areas of agricultural comparative advantage, reinvest the initial profits, and so quickly grow beyond minimum efficient scale. Major successes were registered in a number of sectors, perhaps most notably in aquaculture (shrimps, tilapia). Compare this success to neighbouring Cambodia, which was forced to retain its neoliberal policy parameters under the 'guidance' of the international development community, and as a result has manifestly failed to escape its poverty and underdevelopment through enterprise development (it has instead one of the world's largest microfinance sectors which, of course, is part of the problem). Moreover, even though the current financial structure in Vietnam is evolving to take into account emerging inefficiencies and new development thinking, it has nevertheless managed to remain geared up to the promotion of local economic development rather than simply maintaining or extending its own survivability/profitability. For sure, some elements of this local financial model are unprofitable in a narrow sense (that is, they require funding from higher state institutions), and this is a fact that has caused much anguish in western neoliberal policy-making circles.[18] But the sensible thinking in Vietnam so far is that if the local financial model is working overall – which it clearly is – then any subsidies provided to parts of the local financial structure not able to achieve financial self-sustainability (though they might still be efficient institutions in a technical sense) can simply be offset against the overall net economic and social development gains. By all accounts, it seems better to have a local financial system that clearly facilitates genuinely sustainable development into the longer term, even if it costs the government and community in the short term, than a World Bank-approved market-driven local financial system that effectively undermines the local community and 'succeeds' only in the very narrow sense of achieving its own financial self-sustainability.

CONCLUSION

This chapter has highlighted just a few of the very many important lessons that need to be learned today, in the aftermath of the global financial crisis, if we are to establish a local financial system that works for the bulk of ordinary people, and not just for bankers, investors, speculators and hedge-fund managers. By examining the experiences of both developed and developing countries in the near past, we can very easily identify and unpack examples of local financial systems and institutions that have been very successful in promoting the local enterprise sector. All told, it would seem in order to provide much greater financial support for community-based financial institutions – financial cooperatives, community development banks, credit unions, building societies and social venture capital funds – all of which are local financial institutions that have a very good track record of building a local economy upon the desired foundations of efficiency, equality, sustainability, dignity, accountability, solidarity and democracy.

NOTES

1. Friedrich Von Hayek, *The Road to Serfdom* (Routledge and Kegan Paul, 1944); Milton Friedman, *Capitalism and Freedom* (Chicago: University of Chicago Press, 1962).

2. Dic Lo, 'The Washington Consensus and the China Anomaly', in Kate Bayliss, Ben Fine and Elisa Van Waeyenberge, *The Political Economy of Development: The World Bank, Neoliberalism and Development Research* (Pluto, 2011).

3. Joseph Stiglitz, *Globalization and its Discontents* (Allen Lane, 2002); Ha-Joon Chang, *23 Things They Don't Tell You About Capitalism* (Allen Lane, 2011).

4. Hyman P. Minsky, *Stabilizing An Unstable Economy* (Yale University Press, 1986).

5. Muhammad Yunus, 'Grameen Bank: Organization and Operation', in Jacob Levitsky, ed., *Microenterprises in Developing Countries* (Intermediate Technology Publications, 1989).

6. Milford Bateman, *Why Doesn't Microfinance Work? The Destructive Rise of Local Neoliberalism* (Zed Books, 2010); Milford Bateman, ed., *Confronting Microfinance: Undermining Sustainable Development* (Kumarian Press, 2011); Maren Duvendack et al., *What is the Evidence of the Impact of Microfinance on the Well-being of Poor People?* (EPPI-Centre, Social Science Research Unit, Institute of Education, University of London, 2011).

7. Moreover, it is now increasingly accepted that most microfinance is not even channelled into microenterprises, but into consumption lending instead (see Bateman, *Why Doesn't Microfinance Work?*).

8. Robert Wade, *Governing the Market* (Princeton University Press, 1990).

9. Giacomo Becattini, 'The Marshallian Industrial District as a Socio-economic Notion', in Frank Pyke, Giacomo Becattini and Werner Sengenberger, eds., *Industrial Districts and Inter-firm*

Co-operation in Italy (International Institute for Labour Studies, 1990).

10. Robert Frank and Phillip J. Cook, *The Winner-Take-All Society: Why the Few at the Top Get So Much More Than the Rest of Us* (Free Press, 1995).

11. David Harvey, *The New Imperialism* (Oxford University Press, 2003).

12. David Ellerman, *The Socialisation of Entrepreneurship: The Empresarial Division of the Caja Laboral Popular* (Industrial Cooperative Association, 1982).

13. Piero Ammirato, *La Lega: The Making of a Successful Cooperative Network* (Dartmouth Publishing Company, 1996); see also Stefano Zamagni and Vera Zamagni, *Cooperative Enterprise: Facing the Challenge of Globalization* (Edward Elgar, 2010).

14. Quoted in John Logue, *Economics, Cooperation, and Employee Ownership: The Emilia-Romagna Model – In More Detail* (Ohio Employee Ownership Centre, 2005).

15. Milford Bateman, Juan Pablo Duran Ortīz and Kate Maclean, *A Post-Washington Consensus Approach to Local Economic Development in Latin America? An Example from Medellín, Colombia* (Overseas Development Institute, 2011).

16. Milford Bateman, Juan Pablo Duran Ortīz and Dean Sinković, 'Microfinance in Latin America: The case of Medellín in Colombia', in Bateman, ed., *Confronting Microfinance*.

17. Duncan Green, *From Poverty to Power: How Active Citizens and Effective States Can Change the World* (Oxfam International, 2008).

18. See Marguerite S. Robinson, *The Microfinance Revolution: Sustainable Finance for the Poor* (World Bank, 2001).

4

The Struggle for Meaning

Shaun Chamberlin

Humanity has dramatically changed our world, causing soil fertility depletion, fish depletion, fresh water depletion, climate change, ocean acidification, peak oil, chemical pollution, biodiversity devastation, inequity and war, among other crises. In the face of all this, we are left with what John Holloway memorably characterised as 'the great anguish of *"what can we do?"*'[1]

Suggestions abound, yet somehow it seems that the solutions we choose always cause more problems. Why is this? I suggest that it is because of something fundamental underlying our choices – *our stories*.

THE IMPORTANCE OF STORIES

In human cultures around the world and throughout history, stories have told us what is important and defined our identity. This is why we use fairy stories to educate our children, why advertisers pay such extraordinary sums to present their creations, and why politicians present both positive and negative visions and narratives to win our votes. Stories shape our actions – it only takes an hour to learn how to plant a tree, but it could take a lifetime to see why you might want to.

In the western capitalist culture in which I was raised, the story that humanity exists only to consume the fruits of a world laid out for our convenience retains great influence, and other powerful stories guide us too. The dominance of the story of 'progress' – that we currently live in the most advanced civilisation the world has ever known, and that we are advancing further and faster all the time – makes 'business as usual' an attractive prospect. Why would we not wish to continue this astonishing advancement? And, perhaps most influential of all, our governments entrust key decisions to economic theories which tell stories of the 'invisible hand' of the market, which calmly allocates resources and energy in the best possible way through the divine conjunction of competition, supply and demand, and self-interest.

It seems unbelievable that such stories still hold sway, given the ever more damning scientific understanding of the global impacts humanity's choices are having, but psychologists have long known that our stories are highly resistant to evidence that challenges our world-view and identity.[2] We have so much invested in our stories that it is as though our very self-worth is under threat ('is my chosen lifestyle, or my belief-system, really contributing to the death of our world?'), and we have an arsenal of psychological responses to such threats, reinforced by the relentless, overwhelming *normality* of the mainstream culture all around us. Of course, viewed in a historical context, our modern way of life is anything but typical, but for many of us it is all we have known, and even if we are not comfortable with it, the powerful cultural story that 'real change is impossible' (despite all evidence to the contrary) urges us to accept things as they are. Here, then, lies our fundamental challenge – challenging and changing the stories that define success, identity and meaning in our culture.

Fortunately, we are not alone. There is a vast and diverse upwelling of people, organisations and communities who are acutely aware of the evidence painstakingly collected by the scientists, and are forging new stories that might better serve our collective future. Paul Hawken characterised this self-organising human response as part of the Earth's own immune system, working to counter the very real threat to life on the planet (to us).[3] The mainstream media chooses not to tell us much about these groups, preferring to champion consumerism, but where would any of us be if our own body's immune system got distracted seeking its personal fortune, say, or pursuing hedonistic diversions? The truth is that we are part of the largest movement in the world, which has grown up without name or structure, simply as a response to very human desires for water and food, for justice, for diversity and for health. Above all, for a future.

LOCAL COMMUNITY ACTION – THE TRANSITION MOVEMENT

The strand of this movement that I have been most involved with is the Transition Towns, a network of hundreds of communities around the world (ranging from favelas in Brazil to Japanese towns, from rural villages in England to Transition Los Angeles) unified in their drive to devise and implement positive solutions that build local resilience and reduce fossil fuel dependency. Transition acts on the understanding expressed by one of its key influences, the late Dr David Fleming, 'Localisation stands, at best, at the limits of practical possibility, but it has the decisive argument in its favour that there will be no alternative.'[4]

The practical manifestations of this movement are as diverse as the communities that give birth to them, ranging from food cooperatives, local currencies, skill-sharing sessions and renewable energy projects to Transition Universities, arts projects, the occupation of unused buildings and land, and Energy Descent Action Plans for entire regions, endorsed by local government. But perhaps most importantly, these practical projects are growing out of a new sense of how we should respond to radically changing times. Our culture generally offers two ways of responding to crises – individual action like changing light bulbs or biking instead of driving, and political lobbying of those in power to get changes made. Yet individual action can feel insignificant in the face of global challenges, and political lobbying is often simply ignored. With these the only apparent options, it is easy to see why many become disheartened with activism.

Transition offers one meaningful alternative, and I believe that this is part of the explanation for its ongoing rapid growth. Transition is local communities recognising that the dominant stories in our culture have no future, and grasping the opportunity to profoundly rethink much of what we have come to take for granted. To borrow a phrase from the actor and activist John O'Neal, it is throwing an anchor into the future we want to build, and pulling ourselves along by the chain; taking direct action on a more significant scale than can be achieved alone, yet where individual input remains valued and significant. Perhaps most meaningful of all is the realisation that when communities get together to act, they truly become communities again, rather than just groups of independent individuals. We learn to rely on each other again for some of our needs, rather than on money and the complex systems of the global economy. We get to know each other's strengths and limitations, understand each other's characters, and learn to co-create. So many attempts at recapturing our lost 'community spirit' believe that getting together every Tuesday evening is enough, but it is not. The basis of community is not simply meeting up and being nice to each other, it is truly depending on each other for something that matters.

I have been involved with the Transition movement for five years, as one of the co-founders of Transition Town Kingston, and my book, *The Transition Timeline*, developed the theme of Transition's role as storyteller.[5] The heart of the book is a fleshing out of what we call the 'Transition Vision', which was developed in collaboration with a wide cross-section of Transitioners and others. This presents a response to the despair widespread among those who perceive the severe troubles facing our world, and taps into the powerful motivation that lurks hidden within hopelessness. If despair is perceiving an undesirable future as inevitable, one glimpse of a realistic, welcome alternative transforms our despondency into a massive drive to work towards that alternative. The Transition Vision, then, is of a future in which we create a resilient, more localised society which avoids the worst potential of environmental catastrophe through building thriving lower-energy communities teeming with satisfying lifestyles and fulfilled people. In the book this vision is tracked through a 'history of the next twenty years', and set alongside three other possible futures based on different stories of our place in the world. Some of these might be grounds for despair, *if* they were our only option.

HOW CAN LOCAL SOLUTIONS SCALE UP
TO ADDRESS GLOBAL PROBLEMS?

I believe that the Transition movement represents a powerful force for a better future, as part of the wider movement for a long-term future that is swelling all around us. But we must also recognise that many of our problems are of a global nature, and that such local solutions are necessary but not sufficient. Small-scale solutions can struggle to match up to large-scale problems. With this in mind, Fleming formulated an important principle, 'Large scale problems do not require large-scale solutions – they require small-scale solutions within a large-scale framework.'[6]

This reflects the fact that large-scale solutions too face their own inherent problem – that of disconnectedness. For example, while it is tempting to think of hard-won political agreement on a tightening global cap on emissions as a solution to climate change, such a cap is meaningless without on-the-ground solutions at the local and individual levels. This is, after all, where those emissions are generated. The true challenge lies not in the essential process of agreeing a cap, but in transforming our society so that it can thrive within this limit. If we fail in this, the pressure to loosen or abandon any cap will become irresistible – 'enough talk of future generations, my children are hungry today'.

It is clear that we need the kind of global agreement on climate change put forward in schemes like Contraction and Convergence or Greenhouse Development Rights, which would assign clear national carbon budgets within an adequate global response. And it is clear that we need local responses of the kind that Transition is exploring. Both tasks are the focus of huge energy and determination. What is missing is the bridge between the two. A framework that can encourage and harness those human-scale changes, and ensure that they are adequate to meeting national commitments to reduced emissions. Of course the UK Government (in common with others around the world) has started thinking about this challenge. Indeed, at present it has over a hundred policies that impact on emissions levels. But it has produced, in the words of its own Parliamentary Environmental Audit Committee, 'A confusing framework that cannot be said to promote effective action on climate change.'[7]

TEQS (TRADABLE ENERGY QUOTAS)

One alternative that could provide the necessary cohesive framework is Fleming's TEQs scheme. He first published on the idea in 1996, and it has been the subject of Parliamentary interest since 2004, with a scoping study (2006) and pre-feasibility study (2008) followed by a detailed report from the All Party Parliamentary Group on Peak Oil (2011). In essence, the TEQs scheme is a national energy rationing system which would provide a means to guarantee the achievement of national emissions targets while ensuring fair access to energy and supporting local initiatives like those of the Transition movement. The carbon-rated energy rations would be distributed free of charge to every individual, on an equal *per capita* basis, and the energy-thrifty would be able to benefit from selling their surplus to heavier users. Organisations, the government and all other energy users would buy the units they need to cover their energy purchases at a weekly auction. As a national scheme, it would operate as the smaller-scale system within a larger (global) framework for addressing climate change, while itself providing the larger framework for smaller-scale (local) energy descent plans. It could provide the bridge that we are lacking between local solutions and global problems.

Rationing is seen by many as a dirty word due to its association with shortage, yet it is a response to shortage, not the cause of it. Combining the necessary reductions in the use of high-carbon fuel with the depletion of global energy resources is sure to put increased pressure on energy supplies, and in times of scarcity we cry out for guaranteed fair shares. As the Chairman of the UK Environment Agency has acknowledged, 'rationing is the fairest and most effective way of meeting Britain's legally binding targets for cutting greenhouse gas emissions'.[8] The purpose of TEQs would be to share out fairly the shrinking energy/carbon budget, while allowing maximum freedom of choice over energy use. The alternative is continuing the present arrangement of 'rationing by price' (i.e. the richest get whatever is in short supply), which brings only inequity, suffering and resentment.

Importantly, the TEQs scheme is also built around the principle that we need to move away from a money-focused approach to problems that are not really about money. Our culture's belief in the omniscience of markets has led to a wide range of market-based approaches to addressing climate challenge, based on raising the price of carbon, but this has led to policy working against itself in trying to fulfil the inherently contradictory aims of raising the carbon price and keeping energy prices low. Unsurprisingly, it has also proved hard to gain popular support for increasing the cost of fossil fuels, since people rightly perceive that this increases their cost of living. TEQs offer a fundamentally different approach. Rather than raising the price of carbon/energy and hoping that this reduces demand sufficiently, TEQs constrain the markets within a strict quantity-based carbon budget and allow price to find its level within that. This restores straightforward motivation for individuals, organisations and nations; once you guarantee people a fair entitlement to energy, in line with a declining cap, society can then collectively focus its attention on finding ways to thrive on reduced demand, and thus keep the price of energy/carbon *as low as possible*. This is a simply understood task that everyone can buy into with enthusiasm, and would also resolve the problem that within current economic structures, reducing demand for fossil fuels locally, or even nationally, tends only to reduce the price of these fuels, and thus encourage greater consumption elsewhere.

The essence of TEQs, though, is that it provides a large-scale framework to encourage and empower those local-scale solutions. It effectively converts the national carbon budget into a personal energy budget for everyone, with the clear recognition that this budget will be decreasing year on year. With supply thus fixed, any decreases in national demand lead directly to lower prices for all, making it transparently in the collective interest to work together to find ingenious ways to reduce demand for energy from high-carbon sources (e.g., through lifestyle change or increased supply of low-carbon energy). This cooperation is essential, since the transformation in infrastructures necessitated by climate change requires collaboration between the different sectors of society, united in a single scheme easily understood by all. Policy must encourage constructive interaction between households, businesses, local authorities, transport providers, national government, and so on. In short, the TEQs scheme is explicitly designed to stimulate common purpose in a nation, with the rises and falls in the single national price of the rations providing a clear indicator of how successfully the country is moving towards the shared goal of living happily within our energy and emissions constraints. Additionally, the substantial income from the auction of units to organisations would be accessible to communities to fund the building of new local infrastructure or otherwise support their energy transition.

We may sometimes be tempted to hold fossil fuel companies and governments responsible for all our ills, but it must be recognised that even if they wished to they could not solve our energy problems without the engagement of the wider public. Our individual and community lifestyles need transformation too, and this cannot be done for us. No system can ever relieve us of our personal responsibility, and it is essential that we all recognise the need to change the way we live.

THE STORIES OUR STRUGGLE TELLS

So while Transition takes individuals' solitude and despair and transforms them into communal action, TEQs could combine those community initiatives into an empowered – and sufficient – wave of change at the national level, ready to fulfil global agreements and resolve global challenges. Crucially, neither TEQs nor Transition take the top-down approach of laying out some master-plan that must then be implemented and enforced over any local objections. Both frameworks enable and support creative self-expression and cooperation, but they do not attempt to direct it. As such, they express and support a very different story of our relationship with each other and with our world; a story for which Charles Eisenstein provides a beautiful name. We often speak of 'Mother Earth', and have treated her much as a young child treats its mother – as someone that we can take and take from without consideration for how much she can give. Yet we now know that if this relationship is to be sustained, we must learn to respond to our planet's needs and limits. Eisenstein suggests that we are ready to grow into the story of 'Lover Earth': 'The relationship to a lover is different: to a lover we desire to give as well as to receive, and we desire to create together, each offering our gifts towards a purpose transcending each of us, so that our union becomes greater than the sum of our individuality.'[9]

Perhaps this is the only story that has a future at all. Even if so, this still provides no guarantee that it will come to be told and retold, but as we struggle for meaning in these turbulent times, we must each choose the stories that will be told through our lives and our actions. Let us choose those which make hope possible.

NOTES

1. J. Holloway, *Crack Capitalism* (Pluto, 2010), p. 10.
2. D. K. Sherman and G. L. Cohen, 'The Psychology of Self-defence: Self-affirmation Theory', in M. P. Zanna, ed., *Advances in Experimental Social Psychology*, Vol. 38 (Academic Press, 2006), pp. 183–242, http://is.gd/SsG8hM
3. P. Hawken, *Blessed Unrest: How the Largest Movement in the World Came into Being and Why No One Saw it Coming* (Viking, 2008), p. 141.
4. Quoted in R. Hopkins, 'Building Miles', *Resurgence* 236 (2006), http://is.gd/LivC6H
5. S. Chamberlin, *The Transition Timeline: For a Local, Resilient Future* (Green Books, 2009), http://www.darkoptimism.org/book.html
6. D. Fleming, *Energy and the Common Purpose: Descending the Energy Staircase with TEQs (Tradable Energy Quotas)*, 3rd ed.

(The Lean Economy Connection, 2007), p. 39, http://www.teqs. net/downloads.html

7. Environmental Audit Committee, *Environmental Audit Committee Ninth Report* (House of Commons Parliamentary Press, 2007), http://is.gd/AXuxGr

8. B. Webster, 'Carbon Ration Account for all Proposed by Environment Agency', *The Times*, 9 November 2009, http://www.timesonline. co.uk/tol/news/environment/article6909046.ece

9. C. Eisenstein, 'Rituals for Lover Earth', *Dark Optimism* blog, 16 October 2009, http://www.darkoptimism.org/2009/10/16/rituals-for-lover-earth

Part 2
New Governance

This section explores alternative ways of understanding and practising self-organisation.

Richard Seymour runs through recent examples of self-government of the people, such as the democratic experiment of Tahrir Square in Cairo, and develops an argument in favour of the creation of a 'new model commune'.

Peter Hallward unfolds the notion of the dictatorship of the proletariat – or proletarian democracy – through historical and philosophical examples. In the face of today's political developments, he argues, there are several good reasons to retain this difficult but powerful political concept.

Mark J. Smith opens the problem of government and citizenship to an environmental approach. Through an exploration of the concept of practical utopianism, Smith engages with the possibility of imagining and defining an ecological citizenship.

Marina Sitrin draws on her first-hand experiences and interviews with people in the global Occupy movements. Discussing examples from Argentina, Spain, Greece and the US, Sitrin advocates the importance of horizontalism as a method of self-organisation and of personal development.

5
Towards a New Model Commune

Richard Seymour

What are we fighting for? I think we're fighting for self-govern-ment. I think all of our efforts so far have been a way of saying that we should be collectively in charge of our own lives. I think, whether we conceive it in this way or not, this means trying to move beyond the public; towards a post-public, rather than new publics. This is not just because notions of 'the public realm' are gendered and historically elitist – and by the way, Dan Hind's recent book *The Return of the Public* is an excellent account of this – but because the public-private dichotomy is part of the means by which we are maintained as dependents. As public citizens we exercise a franchise, but in the private sphere we accept bondage: the discipline of the market compels us to accept it. For many, or most, of our waking hours, we cede executive control over our bodily and mental powers to someone else – in the vain hope of one day retiring with a decent pension. Whoops, that's gone. You'll just have to save more. But you'll have to borrow more, because the economy needs you to spend. And we find that in all but the most mundane matters, when it comes to the activities and processes that constitute the major part of our lives, we have no autonomy. We do not govern ourselves.

Even our free time is not really ours. Much of it is spent commuting for a start – the average person's commute is equivalent to four weeks out of a working year. Four weeks – on that tube, that bus, that motorway lane. Think about what that's costing you psychically. Much of the rest is spent recuperating, essentially recovering our ability to labour so that we can go into work and do it all again the next day. And don't forget, of course, that even your free time isn't necessarily your own, because companies now want to organise your fun. Dress-down Friday

– because Friday is funday; birthday parties, and office drinks, team-building outings, sporting days. Your fun, your enjoyment, your affection, often your time – on their orders. Awkward socialisation with middle and senior managers, stressful, moronic conversations, and long-winded explanations of what goes on in different departments that you didn't ask for, and you don't need. Then there's voluntary, unpaid overtime, worth £29 billion a year to the employers – that's called flexibility, and what a good sport you are for doing that.

No more do we govern ourselves in our home lives which all too often become tiny kingdoms, patriarchies in which, among other things, children are acculturated to being ruled by others, and in which the first springs of what I would call 'capitalist guilt' are lodged in place – capitalist guilt is that gut-wrenching anxiety you feel when you're late for work, even though you probably won't get into too much trouble for it; it's the shame that ruins your day when you call in sick, and immediately, absurdly, start to think 'should I go in anyway?'

So, we must be alert to the ways in which, when something beautiful starts to happen, people begin to declare their independence. They begin to run their own lives, to take their rightful part in the running of the whole of society. They exercise their due franchise fully, in every sphere of life. I will not exhaust you with utopian blueprints or detailed analysis of the Paris Commune, or the Russian Revolution, though these repay analysis. But look at the history. In almost every revolution, there are workers' committees, cordones, shuras, soviets, popular councils, cooperatives, collectives, syndicates of some kind, some attempt to work out the protocols for self-government. Even in protest movements and rebellions short of outright revolution, people always confront the problem of how they organise themselves properly, democratically; sometimes that has to confront issues of oppression, including the sexual, gendered or racial oppression that can operate within movements; sometimes it just has to do with developing procedures that genuinely include everyone, avoiding majoritarian tyrannies (this is why in the students' occupations, we've seen experimenta-tion with things like consensus decision-making). In striving towards self-government, towards the commune in other words, we always encounter unanticipated levels of complexity, but the basic problem remains one of self-government.

So, I want to look at the materials that are available to us to flesh out a 'new model commune', and it seems to me that the best starting point is to look at the tendencies immanent in recent struggles in the Middle East. Here, for example, are some of the features of the revolutionary movement that overthrew Mubarak, and even as of Winter 2012 is still fermenting in Egypt. First of all, they took over a nominally public space which the state wished to exclude them from: Tahrir Square. Having taken it over, and affirmed that they wouldn't simply go home at the end of the day – something we might want to think about – they saw off wave after wave of assault on the protests, from police and plain clothes thugs. They set up committees to keep watch for government men. They set up barricades, and routine ID checks for everyone attempting to enter the square. They set up a network of tents for people to sleep in – it's freezing overnight, so some of them jog round the square to get their temperature up. There are toilet arrangements – no small logistical matter when there are routinely hundreds of thousands of people occupying the capital's main intersection. They rig up street lamps to provide electricity. They set up garbage collection, medical stops – they occupy a well-known fast food outlet and turn it into somewhere that people shot at or beaten by police can get treated.

They set up a city within a city, and collectively coped with many more challenges than the average city would have to face in an average day. There was of course commerce, people hawking food and cigarettes, confident that the whole system of exchange wasn't being overthrown. Yet, far more of their actions were driven by solidarity, collective decision-making, and democratic delegation, than is ever usual for a city. Tahrir Square was the beginnings of a commune. Beyond that spectacular exercise in the capital, the labour movement that had been ascendant since 2005 was doing something that labour movement's usually don't do. It was starting to strike to demand a change in management. It was striking over the exercise of authority. This had happened in Tunisia, and usually it was because a company CEO was some ruling party stooge. But it was the people who normally have no say in the running of the company – and Egypt's private sector economy is overwhelmingly informal, and insecure – seeking to exercise a sort of limited franchise. They did not seek to replace the management of the company with themselves, which would have been the ultimate statement of their confidence in their ability to rule themselves. But they were trying to have a say, and usually succeeded in that. And when the government withdrew the police from local communities and encouraged looting and thuggish behaviour, the people – instead of panicking, and deciding they couldn't do without the police after all, so please send the uniformed thugs back in Mr Mubarak – organised self-defence committees. Just as in Tahrir, they set up checkpoints, ID checks, and they made decisions about how their community would be run.

Now, this isn't socialism. Socialists were a current in the revolution, but not a big one. The major currents were Nasserists, Islamists, and liberals. And there are all sorts of political struggles that still have to continue – the horrible attacks on women in Tahrir Square on international women's day show that this fight has to occur within the revolution. Subsequently, the army leadership sought to consolidate a conservative ruling bloc with the assistance of the Muslim Brothers, who were an invaluable part of the revolutionary coalition but always the most right-wing element of it. While many Brothers were shaken up, radicalised and blasted with ecstasy by this revolution, their core base of small businessmen were anxious to get back to making money, and leave the commune behind. This was evident in the ambiguous role played by the Brothers in the re-occupation of Tahrir Square in November 2011. While many rank and file Islamists participated, the position of the leadership tended to support the Supreme Council of the Armed Forces in their attempt to restore 'order'. This ambiguity was again apparent when in December 2011 a leading Muslim Brother sought the prosecution of the Revolutionary Socialists, a far left organisation which had gained a foothold during the revolution, only to abandon it under pressure from a coalition of political parties. Still, the utopian moment of Tahrir Square and beyond showed us some of the lineaments of what a commune might look like. It demonstrated that with opportunity comes competence: that we can, if given the chance, quickly learn and apply the techniques of cooperation, solidarity and self-government.

In response to the student protests in the UK, the British Party of Order – the Tories, the right-wing media, the police, the agents of authority and control – has been most vexed about the challenge posed by the mob, the student protesters. Cameron denounces them as 'feral', and the ideological frame that the media sought to apply – of selfish, solipsistic vandals disrespecting democracy – was ultimately supplied by one totemic incident, that of a fire extinguisher being lobbed from the top of Conservative Party headquarters. This 'mob', they said, clearly doesn't respect democracy. But democracy is not law and order. Democracy is the mob; the mob is democracy.

Democracy is supposed to mean popular sovereignty, not the unimpeded rule of a no-mandate government. It is supposed to mean that the will of the majority governs, not the interests of the rich. It is supposed to mean at minimum that people get the policies they vote for, not those they are overwhelmingly hostile to. In liberal democratic theory, the people are sovereign inasmuch as their aspirations and prerogatives are effectively mediated through a pluralist party-political state. They may not get all that they want all of the time, but the decision-making process will be guided by the public mood, which rival parties must compete to capture and express. Yet this system has only ever been effective, to the limited extent that it has been, when it has been supplemented by militant extra-parliamentary pressure, by the threat of disruption to stable governance and profit-accumulation. To the extent that the parliamentary system is ever really democratic, it is parasitic on a much more fundamental popular democracy. This reality, be it ever remembered, should exhort us to go further than we have, to turn our mobs into committees, shuras, soviets, communes. Let us, in future struggles, pose in practice the material possibility of our self-government.

It is, of course, a long-standing ruling-class prejudice that we cannot govern ourselves. Trotsky once said, perhaps incautiously, that the Russian Revolution was a gamble on the idea that ordinary working-class people could rule themselves, and against the filthy aristocratic prejudice that they could not. His recent biographer, Robert Service, aligns with the Party of Order, insisting that Trotsky was foolish ever to have believed such a stupid thing. No surprises there. Trotsky, and the movements he inspired, hated the Stalinist regime for its savage despotism, the complete lack of genuine autonomy enjoyed by the mass of people. What the Party of Order hate about communism, however, is not what went catastrophically wrong with it, but what is right about it, what is admirable, just, plausible and worth emulating about it. It is the same thing that they hate about us – and we should welcome their hate, and their natural fear. It shows that their right to govern is no longer assured.

6

People and Power: Four Notes on Democracy and Dictatorship

Peter Hallward

Over the course of the last century the word 'democracy' was rendered almost meaningless, at the same time and for many of the same reasons that the term 'dictatorship' was filled with an obscure and deceptive meaning.

The terms themselves are straightforward enough. Democracy means rule of the people, the assertion of the people's will. Democracy applies in so far as the collective will of the people over-powers those who exploit, oppress, or deceive them. Abstracted from such relations of power and over-power, democracy is an empty word.

A good deal of recent discussion about political mobilisation borders a similar emptiness. For several decades now, the prevailing emphasis of theoretical discussion has been on complexity, pluralism, multiplicity, difference, singularity. Suspicion of all general let alone universal terms has itself become general. The priority has been less the consolidation of popular unity and collective purpose than a valorisation of the fragmentary, the disruptive, the ephemeral, the divergent ... The question of power has been left to one side.

In many parts of the world, these same decades have witnessed what is arguably the most dramatic phase of popular disempowerment since the early part of the twentieth century. If much of the twentieth century was shaped by a struggle between capital and labour, between exploiter and exploited, its last quarter was shaped above all by the triumph of capital. The power of those who own and control the means of production is now more coordinated and more absolute than it's been for almost a hundred years. Neoliberal economic 'integration' has reduced the role of most governments, including the most 'democratic', to that of local enforcer of a global class agenda. The spectacular lack of any forceful popular response to the recent conversion of banking-sector losses into public debt (what Naomi Klein denounces as 'the greatest heist of monetary history'[1]) is the most dramatic symptom of a much deeper tendency. Even in a relatively privileged country like the UK, no less a person than the governor of the Bank of England has been impressed, so far, by the degree of popular deference and passivity. 'The price of this financial crisis is being borne by people who absolutely did not cause it', he said on 1 March 2011. 'Now when the cost is being paid, I'm surprised that the degree of public anger has not been greater than it has.'[2]

The capitalist 'democracies' that still dominate the world, needless to say, function less to enable popular empowerment than to accommodate people to their own subjugation. A large part of the strategy underlying such accommodation draws on the old (indeed ancient) demonisation of popular power as itself tyrannical, and thus 'undemocratic'. Fear of an incipient 'tyranny of the majority' is perhaps the most profound motivating force of a liberal tradition conceived in terms broad enough to include Montesquieu, Burke, de Tocqueville and Mill. Perhaps the greatest single achievement of subsequent liberal thought has been to align the 'acceptable' meaning of 'democracy' with an affirmation of the established balance of class forces, such that the very idea of a revolutionary let alone 'dictatorial' democracy can be dismissed as an apparent contradiction in terms.

Lenin's invocation of a 'revolutionary-democratic dictatorship of the proletariat and the peasantry',[3] like Mao's subsequent affirmation of a 'democratic dictatorship of the people',[4] might now seem to belong to a museum of political anachronisms at best, or to a collection of history's greatest crimes at worst. Even the recent revival of a broader academic interest in Marx and in 'the idea of communism' seems to stop short of a line drawn by the still unutterable phrase: the 'dictatorship of the proletariat'.

Marx himself, however, insisted on the practice (rather more than the phrase), and Lenin was characteristically implacable:

'to confine Marxism to the theory of the class struggle means curtailing Marxism, distorting it, reducing it to something acceptable to the bourgeoisie. A Marxist is solely someone who *extends* the recognition of the class struggle to the recognition of the *dictatorship of the proletariat*.'[5] Many years later Etienne Balibar, summarising Lenin's arguments in opposition to the French Communist Party's decision to expunge the phrase from its vocabulary, likewise concluded that insistence on the dictatorship of the proletariat remained an essential part of Marxism. 'The very idea that, in the history and the strategy of the Communist Parties, the dictatorship of the proletariat might be "out of date" can have no meaning for a Marxist. For, as we have seen, the dictatorship of the proletariat is not a particular method, a particular model or a particular "path of transition" to socialism', but rather the name for this transition itself.[6] That was in 1976. Since then, apart from Hal Draper's detailed studies of its history,[7] reference to proletarian or democratic dictatorship has been largely consigned to precisely that – history.

I think there are at least four reasons why it is still worth retaining the notion of a popular or democratic dictatorship in our set of contemporary political concepts.

1

Reference to dictatorship evokes directly and without apology the coercive dimension of revolutionary change, the fact that such change only proceeds in the face of the determined resistance of those opposed to it. As Draper demonstrates at convincing length, by 1844 Marx had reached the conclusion that 'to achieve communist transformation of society, the proletariat first had to conquer political power', and he later accepted the phrase 'dictatorship of the proletariat' as one of several ways of formulating the notion of 'the rule of the working class' or 'conquest of political power by the working class'.[8] As a matter of course, such conquest can only begin (as the *Manifesto* puts it) with 'despotic inroads on the rights of property, and on the conditions of bourgeois production': once the proletariat is powerful enough to expropriate the property of those who exploit them, it 'will use its political supremacy to wrest, by degree, all capital from the bourgeoisie' and thereby assert collective ownership of the means of production.[9] The sort of political power required will depend on the sort of resistance encountered. Some of the measures involved in the formation of such a workers' state would be implemented as early as 1871, by the Paris Commune. The subsequent fate of this experiment also demonstrated, to Marx (and then to revolutionary leaders from Saint Petersburg in 1905 to Shanghai in 1967) the most obvious condition that any such project must meet if it is to endure: acquisition of a capacity to over-power its adversaries.[10]

Like Marat's call for a 'dictator or military tribunal' to be invested with limited and temporary power under the watchful eyes of the people,[11] Lenin's call for proletarian dictatorship is framed by the immediate strategic requirements of the struggle for genuine democracy. If democracy is to expand to become rule of the people as such, i.e. 'democracy for the poor, democracy for the people, and not democracy for the rich, then the dictatorship of the proletariat [must] impose a series of restrictions on the freedom of the oppressors, the exploiters, the capitalists'. Hence Lenin's definition: the dictatorship of the proletariat invests the 'vanguard of the oppressed' with the power it needs to 'suppress the oppressors'.[12]

Framing the issue in the old terms of a 'bourgeois' or 'proletarian' dictatorship thus helps to correct the tendency, encouraged by Foucault and his followers, to think of modern forms of power primarily in terms of 'dispersed' interventions and micropolitical adjustments. It has the virtue of addressing, in the starkest terms, the locus and exercise of the sorts of power at issue in the consolidation of class rule, in the domains of production, employment, finance, the media, education, government, the military-industrial complex, and so on. It offers a way of remembering the obvious fact that in any revolution, the critical moments have been decided by a trial of strength, i.e., by the force of arms or their equivalent (by an arming of the people, by a disarming or dissolving of the army, by a change in the relation between people and army, and so on).[13]

2

By the same token, evocation of the apparently anachronistic notion of a 'proletarian dictatorship', or proletarian democracy, forces reconsideration of the relation between these two categories: proletariat and people. Reactionary politicians have regularly sought to valorise the category of the people (as referent of an orderly community or national harmony) at the expense of the proletariat (as bent on 'sectarian' advantage or anarchic chaos), as if the one could only be thought in exclusion of the other; some of Marx's more dogmatic followers have adhered to the same either-or. Ever since Eduard Bernstein, of course, the history of the more affluent parts of the world has been marked by a series of more or less emphatic *adieux au proletariat*, and no doubt the notion of a class defined in purely socio-economic terms as 'without property' remains more the figure of an underlying tendency than the name of a fixed condition. The *political* issue here, however, concerns the status of popular leadership, dramatised in the role attributed to a popular 'vanguard' or 'front line'. Is 'the people' capable of unity and (self-)direction? Is the people a category of multiplicity and dispersal, or are the people capable of leading the way towards their own self-emancipation? Is the people an essentially amorphous and reactive mass, or is it capable of lending itself a 'leading edge' in its struggle for self-determination?

Here Marx, Lenin and Mao insist on one and the same priority: the 'proletariat' is less a name for a particular sociological occupation or group than for an ongoing process which, conditioned by capitalist development, may unite and eventually empower humanity as a whole.[14] The proletariat constitutes itself, politically, as 'the leading class of the nation', and its tendency defines 'the self-conscious independent movement of the immense majority, in the interest of the immense majority'.[15] Unlike the 'vacillating' petty-bourgeoisie and the diffuse peasantry, the conditions imposed on the proletariat organise and concentrate it in ways that make it capable of informed deliberation, resolute commitment and decisive action.[16] As Lars Lih has recently demonstrated in convincing detail, emphasis on such resolute commitment remains central to the militant conception of practice at work across the whole of Lenin's political life. Lenin stakes everything on the transformative role of 'inspired and inspiring class leadership'. The 'heroic scenario' that sustains the Leninist project assumes an unbroken series of links from proletarian vanguard to labouring humanity in its entirety, such that 'the party activists inspire the proletariat who inspire the Russian *narod* [people] who inspire the whole world with their revolutionary feats'.[17]

So long as the world is governed above all by capitalist exploitation and its ongoing intensification, so then proletarian wage workers, positioned in direct confrontation with those who use or 'employ' them, remain best placed to act as the vanguard of the people as a whole.

Retention of the terms 'dictatorship' and 'proletariat' serves to reinforce the elementary idea, already as emphatic in Rousseau as it will be in Lenin, Trotsky, or Mao, that a general will cannot prevail and endure, the people cannot rule, if they cannot sustain (beyond the differences of priority or tactics that will always animate deliberation and debate) a degree of unity, discipline and clarity of purpose. As Rosa Luxemburg understood better than her Bolshevik contemporaries, however, while proletarian dictatorship is essential to a revolutionary assault on capitalism, such 'dictatorship consists in the *manner of applying democracy*, not in its *elimination*'. It involves 'energetic, resolute attacks upon the well-entrenched rights and economic relationships of bourgeois society, without which a socialist transformation cannot be accomplished'. But 'this dictatorship must be the work of the class, and not of a little leading minority in the name of the class – that is, it must proceed step by step out of the active participation of the masses; it must be under their direct influence, subjected to the control of complete public activity; it must arise out of the growing political training of the mass of the people'.[18]

3

Whatever the name given to its 'leading edge', a genuine or literal 'transition to democracy' involves by definition the direct empowerment of the people as such, the people as a divisive whole. What sort of power, concentration and organisation is required for the people to 'dictate', to those who might exploit or oppress them, the terms of its sovereign will? Presentation of the issue in these apparently archaic terms has the virtue of reminding us of the essential difference between delegation and representation or substitution. Formulation of a popular or general will is a matter of inclusive participation, and every such mobilisation invents or adapts the means of association (councils, clubs, unions, parties...) this requires. Thus associated, the people can indeed delegate 'agents' to execute their will, but for reasons explained by Rousseau they cannot delegate their associating and willing as such.[19] There is a world of difference, as Trotsky remembered more often than not, between a dictatorship that allows people to lead the process of their own self-emancipation, and a dictatorship that *substitutes* itself for the people.[20]

It should go without saying that the metaphorical distance which separates a leading 'vanguard' from a rear-bound 'general staff' is measured by the entire width of the people itself.[21] What is at stake is whether or not people can assemble and impose themselves – be it over the course of a struggle to change the conditions of work, or to win civil rights, or to overcome autocracy... – in such a way as to concentrate their power as the power of 'the' people as such. As even the most superficial glance at their history will confirm, the 'democratic' quality of such struggles is not decided in the first instance by whether or not they represent the passive opinion of a prevailing 'majority'.

What is at stake in the decisive moments of a struggle to impose the rule of the people is less representation of majority opinion per se than a question of popular *power*, a question decided by the relation of forces concentrated in a particular time and place. 'Once a certain threshold of determination, obstinacy and courage has been crossed,' notes Alain Badiou with reference to the recent mobilisations in Tunisia and Egypt, 'a people can indeed concentrate its existence in a public square, an avenue, some factories or a university ... In the midst of [such] an event, the people is made up of those who know how to solve the problems that it imposes on them'[22] – for instance the problems, initially insoluble, involved in mounting a demonstration, holding a square, sustaining a strike, toppling a government, winning a civil war... However universal its prescriptive address, the power at issue in such a popular mobilisation will be unavoidably 'dictatorial', Badiou continues, in so far as its legitimacy is first and foremost a matter of collective self-authorisation rather than of sanctioned representation.[23] Dictatorial mobilisation doesn't simply reflect popular opinion, it clarifies and leads it. More precisely, such mobilisation is the means taken or invented by the leading edge of a people, in so far as resistance draws them into a 'battle of wills'.

4

The old conjunction of democracy and dictatorship (a 'dictatorship of the people') addresses another basic need of any revolutionary conception of power: the need to think together its ordinary (enduring) and exceptional (transitional) exercise, its legal and extra-legal dimensions. The *dictatura* of ancient Rome (the delegation of power to a military leader in order to confront a state of emergency) was routinely praised as a safeguard of public liberty by defenders of the classical republican tradition, for instance Machiavelli or Rousseau;[24] defenders of the revolutionary tradition, by the same token, affirm recourse to exceptional powers in terms that resist any conflation with tyranny, or fascism. Republican dictatorship proceeds as an immanent exception to legal norms; a revolutionary dictatorship takes exceptional measures to impose new norms. In neither case, however, need it contradict the literal meaning of democracy itself. As Rosa Luxemburg understood as well as Lenin, any challenge to a ruling class will always be dismissed as 'premature' and thus criminal or tyrannical.[25] But 'the alternatives before us today', she explained in the climactic month of November 1918, 'are not democracy and dictatorship. They are *bourgeois* democracy and *socialist* democracy. The dictatorship of the proletariat is democracy in a socialist sense', neither more nor less.[26] Although the balance of forces has shifted, the same basic choice persists to this day. The real alternative to a socialist or popular democracy is not dictatorship but oligarchy or aristocracy, and nowhere have genuine democratic movements come under more imperial pressure than in those places – for instance Nicaragua in the 1980s, or Haiti in the 1990s – where they mobilised sufficient power to challenge the coercive machinery of the old status quo.

There is little reason to suspect that the democratic challenges of the coming decades can afford to be less confrontational.

NOTES

1. Naomi Klein, 'Capitalism, Sarah Palin-style', 29 July 2009, http://www.naomiklein.org/articles/2009/07/capitalism-sarah-palin-style

2. Phillip Inman, 'Bank of England Governor Blames Spending Cuts on Bank Bailouts', *Guardian*, 1 March 2011, http://www.guardian.co.uk/business/2011/mar/01/mervyn-king-blames-banks-cuts

3. See for instance, V. I. Lenin, *Two Tactics of Social Democracy in the Democratic Revolution* (1905), in Lenin, *Collected Works*, Vol. 9 (Progress Publishers: 1962), pp. 82–6.

4. Mao Zedong, 'On the People's Democratic Dictatorship', 30 June 1949, http://www.marxists.org/reference/archive/mao/selected-works/volume-4/mswv4_65.htm

5. V. I. Lenin, *The State and Revolution* (1917) in Lenin, *Collected Works*, Vol. 25, p. 412. The canonical reference in Marx is brief: 'Between capitalist and communist society there lies the period of the revolutionary transformation of the one into the other. Corresponding to this is also a political transition period in which the state can be nothing other than the revolutionary dictatorship of the proletariat' (Marx, *Critique of the Gotha Program* [1875], Ch. 4, http://www.marxists.org/archive/marx/works/1875/gotha/ch04.htm). Cf. Marx, letter to Joseph Weydemeyer, 5 March 1852, http://www.marxists.org/archive/marx/works/1852/letters/52_03_05.htm

6. Etienne Balibar, *On the Dictatorship of the Proletariat*, trans. Grahame Lock (NLB, 1976), p. 154. Needless to say, Balibar

continued, 'the dictatorship of the bourgeoisie has no interest – on the contrary – in being called by its real name and understood in terms of its real historical power. To suppress the dictatorship of the proletariat is at the same time to suppress the dictatorship of the bourgeoisie ... *in words*. Nothing could serve it better, in practice' (p. 156).

7. Hal Draper, *Karl Marx's Theory of Revolution, Vol. 3: The 'Dictatorship of the Proletariat'* (Monthly Review, 1986); Draper, *The 'Dictatorship of the Proletariat' in Marx and Engels* (Monthly Review, 1987).

8. Draper, *The 'Dictatorship of the Proletariat' in Marx and Engels*, pp. 22–6. 'For Marx and Engels, from beginning to end of their careers and without exception, "dictatorship of the proletariat" meant nothing more and nothing less than "rule of the proletariat" – the "conquest of political power" by the working class, the establishment of a workers' state in the immediate postrevolutionary period' (p. 26).

9. Karl Marx and Friedrich Engels, *The Communist Manifesto* (1848), Ch. 2, http://www.marxists.org/archive/marx/works/1848/communist-manifesto/ch02.htm

10. Cf. Marx, *The Civil War in France* (1871), Ch. 6, http://www.marxists.org/archive/marx/works/1871/civil-war-france/ch06.htm

11. Jean-Paul Marat, speech of 25 September 1792, National Convention, Paris.

12. Lenin, *The State and Revolution*, in *Collected Works*, Vol. 25: pp. 461–2.

13. See for instance Trotsky, *The Russian Revolution* [1930], trans. Max Eastman (Haymarket, 2008), pp. 88–9, 323–4, 751.

14. See for example, among Marx's earlier works, 'A Contribution to the Critique of Hegel's *Philosophy of Right*: Introduction' (1844); *The Holy Family* (1845), Ch. 4; *The German Ideology* (1845), Pt. 1:D; *The Poverty of Philosophy* (1847), Ch. 2; all available at http://www.marxists.org

15. Marx and Engels, *The Communist Manifesto* (1848), Ch. 2, Ch. 1, http://www.marxists.org/archive/marx/works/1848/communist-manifesto/. 'The Communists', Marx and Engels continue, 'do not form a separate party opposed to other working class parties. They have no interests separate and apart from the proletariat

as a whole'; rather, 'they are on the one hand, practically, the most advanced and resolute section of the working-class parties of every country, that section which pushes forward all others: on the other hand, theoretically, they have over the great mass of the proletariat the advantage of clearly understanding the line of march, the conditions, and the ultimate general results of the proletarian movement' (Ch. 2).

16. Cf. Hal Draper, *Marx's Theory of Revolution, Vol. II, The Politics of Social Classes* (Monthly Review, 1978), pp. 40–8, 295–7, 348–51.

17. Lars Lih, *Lenin* (Reaktion Books, 2011), p. 192, p. 46. Cf. Lih, *Lenin Rediscovered: 'What Is to Be Done?' in Context* (Haymarket Books, 2008). A still more 'heroic' scenario, of course, underlies Trotsky's comparable conception of things.

18. Rosa Luxemburg, *The Russian Revolution* (1918), Ch. 8, http://www.marxists.org/archive/luxemburg/1918/russian-revolution/ch08.htm

19. Jean-Jacques Rousseau, *Social Contract* IV, Ch. 1; cf. III, Ch. 15.

20. In 1904 Trotsky feared that Bolshevik methods might encourage the revolutionary party to impose itself in the place of the proletariat, and then 'lead to the Party organisation "substituting" itself for the Party, the Central Committee substituting itself for the Party organisation, and finally the dictator substituting himself for the Central Committee' (Trotsky, *Our Political Tasks* [1904], Pt. 2, http://www.marxists.org/archive/trotsky/1904/tasks/ch03.htm). As Isaac Deutscher points out, the measures that in 1920–21 Trotsky himself took or advocated regarding the coercive 'militarisation of labour' themselves helped paved the way for the very substitution he otherwise feared (Deutscher, *The Prophet Armed* [1954] [Verso, 2003], pp. 421–35).

21. Cf. Peter Hallward, 'Fanon and Political Will', in Nigel Gibson, ed., *Living Fanon: Global Perspectives* (Palgrave Macmillan, 2011), pp. 213–24.

22. Alain Badiou, 'Tunisie, Egypte: quand un vent d'est balaie l'arrogance de l'Occident', *Le Monde*, 18 February 2011, http://www.lemonde.fr/idees/article/2011/02/18/tunisie-egypte-quand-un-vent-d-est-balaie-l-arrogance-de-l-occident_1481712_3232.html

23. Alain Badiou, 'Que signifie "changer le monde"? Séminaire d'Alain Badiou (2010–2011)', 16 March 2011, http://www.entretemps.asso.fr/Badiou/10–11.htm

24. Niccolò Machiavelli, *Discourses On the First Ten Books of Titus Livius*, Ch. 34; Rousseau, *Social Contract* IV, Ch. 6.

25. Rosa Luxemburg, *Reform or Revolution*, in *The Essential Rosa Luxemburg*, ed. Helen Scott (Haymarket Books, 2008), pp. 95–6. The later argument between Luxemburg and Lenin, subsequently reinforced by Lukács, turns on the amount of deliberate and concentrated power required to impose such a transition in unfavourable conditions. Cf. Georg Lukács, 'Critical Observations on Rosa Luxemburg's "Critique of the Russian Revolution"' (1922), in *History and Class Consciousness*, trans. Rodney Livingstone (MIT Press, 1971), pp. 275–8, 283.

26. Rosa Luxemburg, *Ausgewählte Reden und Schriften*, Vol. II (Berlin, 1955), p. 606, cited in Tony Cliff, *Rosa Luxemburg* (1959), section 7, http://www.marxists.org/archive/cliff/works/1959/rosalux/7-bolpower.htm#f75

7
Practical Utopianism
and Ecological Citizenship

Mark J. Smith

UTOPIAN AS PRACTICAL?

In early modern utopian thinking, the constructions of utopians were designed to provide imaginative constructs of what societies could be like if they addressed the prevailing problems of direct experience. For example, Thomas More's seminal *Utopia* (1516) offers a vision of society and the political system that addresses what he considered to be the frailties of the Elizabethan society he inhabited. In some ways, it is backward looking, creating a vision of a simpler division of labour, where occupations and housing are interchangeable and circulated, ignoring the inexorable path towards more complex circuits of differentiated responsibility that feature in modern societies. In particular, the island of Utopia retains common land, with no land enclosed, a key cause of rural poverty in the sixteenth and seventeenth centuries. The focus on reclaiming common ground as a basis for controlling labour power can also be seen in radical experiments such as that of the Diggers, in Cobham, Surrey. Some contemporary critical realists, such as Andrew Sayer,[1] have also talked of a return to a simpler division of labour in their account of moral economies, as do some deep ecology accounts of an ecologically sensitive localised future (Naess; Devall and Sessions).[2]

Marx and Engels, inspired by the French communist Saint-Simon and indirectly by anarchist challengers such as Proudhon and Bakunin, grounded their utopianism in the concrete realities of class-based societies. Their description of the Paris Commune's brief existence in 1870–71 before its violent military suppression by the monarchist armies of Europe was a working model, an experiment in institutional innovation. In place of both monarchism and the representative democracy of the English type, the communards constructed a system of direct democracy. Rather than having political representatives acting according to their perceived national or public interest and thus unaccountable until the subsequent election (the Burkean role for Members of Parliament), elected officials in the Commune were revocable at any time. In addition, many state positions normally reserved for career bureaucrats such as lawyers and judges, or army officers, were also subject to the same rules. In place of the standing army, loyal to its officer class and a supreme government authority, the communards constructed armed militias of the people.

Some attempts to replicate the principles of the commune by later Marxists can be seen in the early operation of Workers' and Peasants' Soviets in Russia or the factory councils of Turin and Milan before the suppression of workers' participation in the 1920s. However, it should be noted that Marx did not attempt to define the specifics of a communist society, but merely identified what must be absent for it to be a successive stage after capitalism – capturing the material abundance of capitalism but eliminating 'economic exploitation' and 'bourgeois domination'. Marx's communism is defined by the absence of waged labour-employer relations and the end of the institutional separation of economy from the superstructure of politics and ideology. For Marx, people make history – it cannot be easily predicted or planned out in advance.

There were a variety of experimental lived utopias that we would now describe as cultural laboratories of lifestyles that can be seen in reaction to the negative side effects of industrialisation and rational bureaucracy.[3] Rather than a vague reference to the proletariat as a political subject, in these projects for personal as well as political and economic change, these utopians explicitly focused on transformation in everyday life and the virtues of certain acts. These kinds of experiments can be seen from William Morris' *News From Nowhere* (1890) and Edward Carpenter's free love movement through to the 1960s communes, women's movement and green utopias (usually combining ecological insights with anarchist principles of social organisation). Like Engels and Eleanor Marx, Morris also focused on the importance of creative and useful labour as a key component of a utopian society. Morris tied this vision to the importance of craftsmanship through the Arts and Crafts movement, while Carpenter tied socialist alternatives to sexual freedom (as a challenge to the conventional structures of marriage).

The cultural revolt of the 1960s took this focus on the personal as a political act into group-based and sometimes community-based activism. The aims of such movements linked personal transformation to social reorganisation – for example feminist activism combined general attacks on discrimination and sexism, specific campaigns against sexual violence, and group consciousness-raising where the perspective of the few is recognised as the common experience of many.

THE ENVIRONMENTAL CHALLENGE

Environmental movements also began to be established in the late 1960s and 1970s, in response to the effects of industrialisation and twentieth-century hazards such as DDT, dioxins, PCBs and nuclear waste materials. Activists questioned economic growth as a measure of human progress. Some established alternative communities rooted in a specific ecological biome, or smaller plots of land, and opted for self-sufficiency as a post-materialist answer to western lifestyles. Like Thomas More, these communities often challenged mainstream ideas of property and consumerism. Anti-militarism was also a distinctive feature, since ecological ideas and peace movements were closely aligned.

The first pictures of the earth from space also provided a provocative demonstration of the fragility of the earth and its limits, both in terms of its capacity to absorb pollution and the availability of exploitable resources. For the early ecological thinkers of the last century, in an oppositional frame of reference, the problem was the military-industrial complex that shored up western capitalism. Over time, the 1980s and 1990s provided a series of examples of technologies that could either provide an alternative to the effects of industry or at least mitigate some of its worst consequences. It became clear how it will be ultimately necessary to rely on technological solutions to carbon dependence for energy production and mobility. However, even if 'technofixes' should not be ignored, it is equally important not to place too much credit at the door of ecological modernisation and of the creation of more sustainable product life-cycles in the corporate responsibility agenda.[4]

In fact, many of the improvements in environmental quality in developed societies have not been the direct result of technology but simply the exportation of environmental degradation across space (to the end of the global supply chain where governance can be poor and regulation weak) and time (the temporary storage of waste from chemical and nuclear facilities with enormous costs that will be borne by our immediate successors or more distant future generations). Even carbon sequestration, the latest large-scale technofix for addressing climate change, could have severe implications for future generations that we may not be able to anticipate. We only have to look at cases such as Windscale, Three Mile Island, Chernobyl and Fukushima to realise that there may be a law of unanticipated consequences that applies to all attempts at nuclear fission as an energy source, and that civil nuclear power was only underwritten politically in its early stages because it provided the materials necessary for weaponisation (the inverse of 'atoms for peace'). Such risks, of course, are not only volatile and subject to considerable vagaries of human error and malevolence, they are insidious, creeping and pay no respect to arbitrary boundaries, such as territorial frontiers. Security, if it makes sense at all in a vulnerable world, is shared.[5] It is with this in mind that we shall now turn to one of the most important practical utopians of our time.

DIAGNOSIS AND PROGNOSIS: BECK'S PRACTICAL UTOPIANISM

Ulrich Beck's account of the transition from an industrial to a risk society also operates a practical utopian logic, presenting a diagnosis of current problems and attempts to think through what alternatives we have in addressing the future. Considering the 'Risk Society' (Risikogesellschaft) suggested that the hazards generated by technological knowledge can be anticipated, but that such problems cannot be easily addressed, as well as that technical solutions on their own are likely to be inadequate.[6] Beck argued that the earlier kinds of development generated risks that were localised and calculable, so the causes of a specific problem could be identified and blame appropriately attached, particularly if a specific company or industrial sector were involved. This was evident for carbon-based carcinogens where regular contact with some materials increased the likelihood of cancer; for example, as early as the eighteenth century with chimney sweeps, and later with bladder cancer following exposure to chemical dyes, through to the effects of radium, x-rays and smoking. Even here, the actual costs of these externalities were not easily accepted into the cost-benefit calculus of the economists' vision of extraction, manufacturing and distribution that resulted from business decisions.

Over time, the effects of industrial processes in polluting water and air became widely associated with cancers, respiratory diseases, immune disorders, digestive illnesses, liver damage and birth deformities. In many cases, direct involvement in the productive processes or proximity to industrial sites provided a tangible basis for linking cause and effect, establishing clearer lines of responsibility. On environmental risks, for example, the fuel economy was regulated to ensure smokeless fuels were used in urban areas, addressing the problem of urban 'smogs'. Similarly, in policy areas such as welfare and private insurance, a 'safety state' emerged by the mid twentieth century, where clear rules of conduct existed for attributing causal responsibility for harm, support in the face of a disaster, and the awarding of compensation for those who experienced the harsh effects of the vagaries of the market system.

Yet, harm and risk are increasingly unattributable, as many negative effects on lives are the culmination of several processes working together without it being necessarily possible to identify a clear single cause, while transboundary spread also generates problems in international coordination and acceptance of responsibility. This is the case, for example, with climate change, toxic chemicals, nuclear waste, acid rain, nonylphenols and other hormone disrupters, heavy metal accumulation in fisheries, and so on.

Initially, Beck focused on environmental impacts, arguing that their complexity, fluidity and unanticipated consequences means that even with scientific management no guarantees exist, that 'victims cannot be specified or determined in advance'.[7] He develops this into a critique of the 'organised irresponsibility' of political decision-makers in contemporary developed societies – of the subtle ways in which elite groups fail to acknowledge the seriousness of the problems they face as well as how scientific knowledge leads to the treatment of danger as normal (as outlined by C. Wright Mills, in the closing passages of his *The Power Elite* [1956]). In short, the enormous risks associated with human activities are translated into acceptable costs, concealing the tremendous hazards. Beck sketches two possible futures in response to the risk society, other than blindly continuing in the same way.

1. Authoritarian technocracy, where strong states use increasingly authoritarian measures to control the likelihood and effects of potential hazards, as seen by the social democratic 'health and safety state' in the name of national environmental, economic and military security. In this scenario, rationality would tame industrialism and each batch of regulations and legislative measures would extend state control and centralise power in the hands of those who control knowledge and expertise.

2. Ecological democracy, where social and political institutions are transformed through citizen participation, greater transparency and accountability. Technological change would only be allowed after a thorough discussion of its possible consequences (rather than being imposed from above) and potential polluters and resource extractors would have to prove the safety of productive processes, rather than those afflicted having to prove that they have been adversely affected (a transformed basis for proof in the legal rules of environmental risk assessment).

Thus, ecological democracy in utopian fashion negates the assumptions of existing practices and in some small way goes beyond the precautionary principle. In many ways, ecological democracy fits in well with the new language of corporate citizenship where constituencies previously ignored in consultation are brought into consideration as stakeholders. Similarly, it parallels the 'just sustainabilities' literature where communities decide on the priorities in planning urban landscapes that are both affordable and ecologically sensitive, an argument picked up and developed by Andrew Light when considering urban ecological citizenship.[8]

BEYOND RISK TO ECOLOGICAL CITIZENSHIP

This narrative of the move from industrial to risk society can be questioned in two ways, which result from the context of its emergence.

1. There is considerable evidence that developed societies still have numerous localised causes of harm. For example, for over one hundred years landfill sites have been built upon, often with public housing. In addition, the dumping and transportation of harmful materials or LULUs – Locally Unwanted Land Uses such as the storage facilities for toxic waste – has often followed the line of least resistance. As a result, it is often those communities with the least active citizenry that are the most vulnerable to local pollution.[9]
2. The most damaging forms of industrial pollution have not been eliminated, merely moved elsewhere, into developing societies. As such, the west or developed nations can only be described as post-industrial in the sense that the negative effects of industry have been redistributed on a global basis. Countries which specialise in capital goods production, financial services, microelectronics and culturally creative industries still need raw materials transformed into goods first.[10]

The risk society approach is open to question, since the exportation of labour exploitation, environmental degradation and questionable technologies from the developed to the less regulated developing world still means that the old risks are relevant. In addition, rapid development and modernisation in some developing countries, without an equitable distribution of the benefits, can raise its own difficulties and possibly generate major social and political conflicts.[11]

However, Beck does usefully explore the contemporary meaning of global risks.[12] Environmental crises such as those associated with climate change and financial risks are portrayed as the 'contingent side effects of decisions in the process of modernisation'.[13] In addition he accepts that older risks such as industrial hazards and war, as well as natural disasters such as earthquakes, are becoming more intertwined with these new forms of global or world risk. Developing countries are thus often confronted with transboundary risks from global (such as climate change) and regional effects (such as air pollution across Southeast Asia), as well as local risks from power generation, toxic chemicals, oil and gas refining, mining, and metal smelting.

These brief examples highlight also how the combination of risks and the intensity and scale of multiple vulnerabilities depend on empirical context. This is why ecological citizenship could provide a useful benchmark for developing 'greenprints' for change which would be based on research into the context of application, as opposed to blueprints that specify rigid and universal solutions in concrete circumstances where old risks, natural disasters and new global risks interact and possibly intensify the effects of each. As Mouffe argues, we need to move from the slippery slopes of total grasp to the rough ground of concrete circumstances.[14]

CITIZENSHIP AS ECOLOGICAL?

Citizenship has traditionally been associated with membership of states, the regulation of migration and the education of younger or newer members of society into the rules and expectations of the nation state. Since the 1990s, however, citizenship has also been a key space of ideological and analytical contestation creating spaces for new forms of identity construction and social transformation projects. Gender, culture, multiculturalism, race, transnationalism, cosmopolitanism, technology and science have all been refracted through the lenses of these new forms of citizenship, all challenging citizenship in its canonised form through varied acts, in different sites and across many scales.[15] This is not the place for a thorough discussion of citizenship studies, but one aspect needs highlighting, namely the reconfiguration of 'politics' into 'the political'. If we are to understand the 'ties that bind' and the 'ties that bond' us together in lived experience, our forms of life and the emotional feelings that are articulated through different social positions are as relevant as the partial aspects of identities that are hailed by party membership, associational membership and citizen acts. This means that the antagonisms and conflicts in political spaces are domesticated through politics imposing a sense of order and organisation, so that enemies become adversaries and even friends on occasion. Citizen subject positions are thus provisional respites, enabling challenges to other subject positions at work, in this case in environmental discourses.

Along those lines, ecological citizenship challenges the assumption that citizenship is

1. territorial and limited to a specific geographic space;
2. contractual where all actors have exclusive rights and duties to each other;
3. concerned primarily with rights, leaving obligations and duties as residual categories;
4. limited to members of (a sub-category of) the human species;
5. concerned with the public sphere rather than the power relations of private life;
6. primarily political, civil and social;[16]
7. primarily concerned with contracts and the ties that bind, to the exclusion of morality, compassion and the ties that bond;[17]

8. defined by a Eurocentric tradition that is also potentially orientalist.

The practical utopianism of ecological citizenship suggests that national territories are less relevant when risks are spread across countries and globally, and it is possible that obligations to others (distant and future strangers) exist when those affected by us do not have rights in our own communities. Obligations and their formalised expression as duties (such as the duty of care) are as relevant if not more so than rights and entitlements, and we also have obligations to consider other non-human species. Citizenship has been tied to rights in civil, political and social contexts, but power relations also operate in private life questioning the liberal distinction between state and civil society – the personal is political and 'greenprints' require changes in private life if they are to succeed. Emotions and the cultivation of virtues to link self-improvement to collective outcomes are also essential, with the distinction between the ties that bind and those that bond of little relevance in the search for practical solutions. Moreover, ecological citizenship could originate in varied forms outside the European context.[18]

Practical utopianism demands we recognise that solutions in one location could have adverse effects elsewhere, and that this applies on a global scale taking account of the full range of environmental issues and the search for solutions that address both social and environmental justice. So, we need to start from a new set of questions in future research: If utopianism were practical what would it look like? If ecological citizenship comes into being, what political subjects could invest their identities in it? What kind of new institutional settlement could practical utopianism and ecological citizenship bring into being? And, globally, can there be a post-orientalist form of ecological citizenship?

NOTES

1. A. Sayer, 'Liberalism, Marxism and Urban and Regional Studies', *International Journal of Urban and Regional Research*

19:1 (1995), pp. 79–95; 'Reply to Gough and Eisenschitz', *International Journal of Urban and Regional Research* 21:1 (1997), pp. 129–32.

2. A. Naess, 'The Shallow and the Deep, Long Range Ecology Movement', *Inquiry* 16 (1973), pp. 95–100; B. Devall and G. Sessions, *Deep Ecology* (Peregrine Books, 1985).

3. See A. Melucci, *Nomads of the Present: Social Movements and Individual Needs in Contemporary Society* (Radius, 1989).

4. A. Mol, 'Ecological Modernisation and Institutional Reflexivity: Environmental Reform in the Late Modern Age', *Environmental Politics* 5:2 (1996), pp. 302–23.

5. See B. S. Turner, *Vulnerability and Human Rights* (University of Pennsylvania Press, 2006); I. Wilkinson, *Risk, Vulnerability and Everyday Life* (Routledge, 2010).

6. U. Beck, *Risk Society: Towards a New Modernity* (Sage Publications, 1992); *Ecological Politics in an Age of Risk* (Polity Press, 1995).

7. Beck, *Ecological Politics in an Age of Risk*, p. 10.

8. A. Light, 'Urban Ecological Citizenship', *Journal of Social Philosophy* 34:1 (2003), pp. 44–63.

9. M. J. Smith and P. Pangsapa, *Environment and Citizenship: Integrating Justice, Responsibility and Civic Engagement* (Zed Books, 2008).

10. M. J. Smith, 'Risk and Vulnerability', in M. Butcher and T. Papaioannou, eds., *International Development in a Changing World* (Bloomsbury Press, 2012).

11. M. J. Smith and P. Pangsapa, 'Clusters of Injustice: Human Rights, Environmental Sustainability and Labour Standards', in H. Yanacopulos and A. Voiculescu, eds., *The Business of Human Rights: An Evolving Agenda for Corporate Responsibility* (Zed Books, 2011).

12. U. Beck, *World Risk Society* (Polity Press, 1999); *Power in a Global Age* (Polity Press, 2005); *World at Risk* (Polity Press, 2009); B. Adam, U. Beck, and J. van Loon, eds., *The Risk Society and Beyond* (Sage Publications, 2000).

13. Beck, *World at Risk*, pp. 13–14.

14. C. Mouffe, *On the Political* (Routledge, 2005).

15. E. Isin and G. M. Nielsen, 'Introduction: Acts of Citizenship', in E. Isin and G. M. Nielsen, eds., *Acts of Citizenship* (Zed Books, 2008).

16. As outlined by T. H. Marshall, *Citizenship and Social Class, and Other Essays* (Cambridge University Press, 1950).

17. As outlined by A. N. H. Dobson, *Citizenship and the Environment* (Oxford University Press, 2003).

18. See Smith and Pangsapa, *Environment and Citizenship*.

8

Occupy: Making Democracy a Question

Marina Sitrin

EMERGENCY BREAKS AND NOW TIME

'Marx says that revolutions are the locomotive of world history. But perhaps it is quite otherwise. Perhaps revolutions are an attempt by the passengers on the train – namely, the human race – to activate the emergency break.' Walter Benjamin's words, written decades ago, resonate perfectly with what has been going on across the globe and throughout the past 15 years, and particular so in 2011.

When the Zapatistas emerged in Chiapas, Mexico, in 1994, they declared a resounding '*Ya Basta*!' (Enough!), and rather than making demands on institutional power, they created dozens of autonomous communities, with their own forms of directly democratic governance, on land they have taken back. In Argentina in 2001, the popular rebellion sang '*Que Se Vayan Todos! Que No Quede Ni Uno Solo!*' (Everyone Must Go! Not Even One Should Remain!). Like the Zapatistas, the Argentinean movement focused on the active creation of horizontal assemblies, rather than on asking formal power to change things. Creating that alternative in the present and in their new social relationships – by taking over and running hundreds of workplaces without bosses, by retaking the land as well as the media, by creating new collectives and cooperatives that broke from past hierarchical ways of relating, they created in their present new types of social relationships and formed a new dignity. 2011 witnessed similar movements around the world, with millions refusing to remain passive in an untenable situation and pulling the emergency break. Still today, in those spaces, in our various towns, villages, cities and countries, we continue creating new social relationships, new ways of being. At the heart of this process, is the retaking of democracy.

This chapter will explore these new social relationships, position them in relation to concepts of democracy, de-linking democracy and capitalism, base these concepts in recent movements from the US to Greece and Spain, and then ground them in the autonomous movements that arose in Argentina in 2001.

HORIZONTALIDAD AND DIRECT DEMOCRACY

Horizontalidad, horizontality, and horizontalism are words that encapsulate the relationships upon which many of the new global movements are grounded – from Spain and Greece, to the US Occupy movement. *Horizontalidad* is a social relationship that implies, as its name suggests, a flat plane upon which to communicate. *Horizontalidad* necessarily implies the use of direct democracy and the striving for consensus, processes in which attempts are made to ensure that everyone is heard and new relationships are created.

Horizontalidad is a new way of relating, based on affective politics and opposed to all the implications of 'isms', despite being sometimes translated as horizontalism. It is a dynamic social relationship, and thus the meaning in English is more than just horizontal or horizontality – there is not yet a perfect word in English to describe this phenomenon. Horizontalism is not an ideology or a political programme that must be met so as to create a new society or a new idea. It is a break with all sorts of vertical ways of organising, and a break which is simultaneously an opening. Horizontalism is not a 'thing' but a process, a way of creating new forms of relating, and, as the forms of relating necessarily change throughout the process, it is also an ever-changing process.

THE INCOMPATIBILITY OF DEMOCRACY AND CAPITALISM

The intention behind the use of *horizontalidad* is not to determine 'the' path that a country should take, but to create the space for a conversation in which all can participate and in which all can determine together what the future should look like, while at the same time attempting to prefigure that future society in present social relationships. At its best, *horizontalidad* is a tool for real democracy.

In fact, one of the most powerful things the global movements achieved in 2011 was to make democracy a question. This is seen in particular in Spain, Greece, the US and parts of Europe. We refuse the privileging of economic interests over political and social ones. What the movements declare is 'Democracy First!' 'We are the 99%' and 'Democracía Real Ya!' This is not how the systems of 'democracy' we live under function. Under capitalism, decisions are made by those with economic power, related to issues of property and the economy, and then the political follows – of course following here really does mean follow. It is a privileging and hierarchising of the economic interests of the few over the interests of the majority. The Occupy movements turn this on its head and say – No! First comes democracy, first people decide! And this is inseparable from economic and social issues. That is the slogan of the 99%. It is a framework of the majority, within which the people lead. Yet, how and what that looks like is still a question.

Amador from the 15M explains this process from the experiences of the movements in Spain:

> The force of the slogan, Democracía Real Ya!, as with other slogans, like 'they say we have democracy and we don't' – is to reflect that we do not live in a democracy, but in a 'dictatorship' of the corporations … Now, in the movement, we have begun the process of discussing what democracy is. Democracía Real Ya! is something we are not totally clear on, and something we are thinking about together. Some speak of direct democracy, others of democracy of the assemblies, and others that maybe we could have a different sort of representative democracy. Democracía Real Ya! has opened a space for so many people who were frustrated with what we have. But what that means is still not clear… (Conversation in 2012, Madrid.)

One thing in common around the globe is that these people creating new democratic forms are not asking their governments to be more democratic. They are inherently outside the framework of institutional power. The implicit argument is that democracy is not possible as long as it is linked to a form of exchange based on hierarchy, inequality, oppression and exploitation. People cannot be physically or emotionally free as long as there is a structural hierarchy deciding those things that are most fundamental to their very working and living. Capitalism and democracy are incompatible. This is not to say that there is opposition to reforms. What it does mean, for example, is that instead of proposing legislation or getting behind a candidate who is against foreclosures (as one is supposed to do in a representative democracy), the movements in Spain and the US are disrupting foreclosure proceedings and occupying people's homes so they are not evicted. In Greece they are occupying the cashiers of the hospitals so that people do not have to pay the newly imposed costs of health care, or refusing to pay bus fare or road tolls. Sometimes the result of this is that laws are changed or rules modified, but the point of the movements is to create new ways of relating – not looking to institutional power, but instead creating power.

This power being created does not accept the value system of capitalism, where the market determines the worth of a person's house or bodily health. This is not to say that the movements identify themselves as explicitly anti-capitalist: what they are doing is refusing to participate in the capitalist logic. The movement logic is that of taking care of one another, and is grounded in prefigurative forms of democracy. This is a different value system than the one based on values determined by the market and on relationships of exchange, as it is based on solidarity and a real democracy decided by people together. These new relations break with capitalist production and create new values. The 'rule' of the movements is not the accumulation of capital or surplus, but that of affect and of networks of solidarity and friendship. This new value is apparent on the subjective level, in people seeing themselves as new, and as changed, and in their liking this newfound agency and protagonism, which is then reflected in their relationships to one another. This new value is also very concrete in that people are finding new ways to survive, to stay housed, and are helping others survive on the basis of these relationships.

ON THE NEWNESS OF THE NEW

What has been taking place around the world since 2011 is new – it feels new, and upon asking almost any participants one would find that they perceive it as a totally new movement. Probably, they will also say that they have changed and that, for the first time, they feel like they have a voice and are heard, and they might even say something about how they feel they are creating real democracy. While true, this does not come without precedents, as similar experiences have occurred, and sentiments been expressed, throughout history and around the globe. To glance briefly at the history of social movements in the US, we can see the importance of the consensus process in the radical feminist and anti-nuclear movements, or the seeking of a 'beloved community' with the Southern Non-Violent Coordinating Committee (SNCC), or even in the early twentieth century with the Industrial Workers of the World desiring to 'create the new in the shell of the old'. We follow in inspiring footsteps, from which we can learn a great deal. These forms, and the desire to prefigure a new world in our relationships now, is global and historical – yet that does not take away the feeling of its newness and of that of its current and variegated permutations. Walter Benjamin wrote that history and the present are a 'secret rendezvous between past generations and our own' (Second Thesis on the Philosophy of History).

The February 2012 issue of Adbusters ran an article that began with the following quotation:

> We began learning together. It was a sort of waking up to a collective knowledge, rooted in a self-awareness of what was taking place in each of us. First we began asking questions of ourselves and each other, and from there we began to resolve things together. Every day we keep discovering

and constructing while we walk. It's like each day there's a horizon that opens before us, and this horizon doesn't have any recipe or program. We have discovered that strength is different when we are side by side, when there is no one telling you what you have to do, and when we're the ones who decide who we are.

It is followed by another similar passage, and then at the very end it is revealed that these quotes are not from the US or Canadian Occupy Movements or from Spain or Greece either, but from Argentina, after the 2001 popular rebellion.[1] The similarities in the autonomous movements in Argentina, from which we get the word *horizontalidad*, and the movements today are so remarkable that they require study, so as to learn both from the inspiring processes of social creation, and from the way they decided to take on, or not, their many challenges.

ARGENTINA 2001–TODAY

The rebellion in Argentina came in response to a growing economic crisis that had already left hundreds of thousands without work and many thousands hungry. The state provided no possible way out. In the days before the popular rebellion, in early December 2001, the government froze all personal bank accounts, fearing a run on the banks. In response, first, one person, then, another, and then hundreds, thousands, and hundreds of thousands took to the streets, banging pots and pans, *cacerolando*. They were not led by any party, and were not following any slogans, they merely sang, '*Que Se Vayan Todos! Que No Quede Ni Uno Solo!*' Within two weeks, four governments had resigned, the Minister of the Economy being the first to flee.

People who had been out in the streets *cacerolando* describe how, during the days of the popular rebellion, they found themselves, found each other, looked around at one another, introduced themselves, wondered what was next, and began to ask questions together.

One of the most significant things about the social movements that emerged in Argentina after the 19th and 20th of December is how generalised the experience of *horizontalidad* was and still is: from the neighbourhood assemblies of the middle class, to those of the unemployed, to workers taking back their workplaces. *Horizontalidad*, and a rejection of hierarchy and political parties was the norm for thousands of assemblies, taking place on street corners, in workplaces and throughout the unemployed neighbourhoods. And now, more than ten years later, as people come together to organise, the assumption is that it will be horizontal, from the hundreds of assemblies currently occurring up and down the Andes fighting against international mining companies, to the thousands of *Bachilleratos*, alternative high school diploma programmes organised by former assembly participants and housed in recuperated workplaces.

Horizontalidad is a living word, reflecting an ever-changing experience. Months after the popular rebellion, many movement participants began to speak of their relationships as horizontal, in order to describe the new forms of decision-making. Years after the rebellion, those continuing to build new movements speak of *horizontalidad* as a goal as well as a tool. All social relationships are still deeply affected by capitalism and hierarchy, and thus by the sort of power dynamics it promotes in all collective and creative spaces, especially in reference to the way people relate to one another in terms of economic resources, gender, race, access to information, and experience. As a result, until these fundamental social dynamics are overcome, the goal of *horizontalidad* cannot be achieved. Time has taught us that, in the face of this, simply desiring a relationship does not make it so. But the process of *horizontalidad* is a tool for the achievement of this goal. Thus *horizontalidad* is desired, and is a goal, but it is also the means, the tool, for achieving this end.

December 19 and 20, 2001, was a crack in history upon which vast political landscapes unfolded. *Qué Se Vayan Todos!* was a song of affirmation. In those defining days of the Argentinean crisis, movements were born, as people united in collective kitchens, art and media collectives, reclaimed workplaces, and indigenous and unemployed movements. Each group used and stressed horizontalism as a social relationship.

In communities across the country, people came together, began to speak and really hear each other, and together ask questions. And this is how the first neighbourhood assemblies were formed. 'People simply met on a street corner in their neighbourhood, with other neighbours who had participated in the *cacerolazos*', said Pablo, a participant in the Colegiales neighbourhood assembly in Buenos Aires.

In Madrid, Ayelen described something almost identical happening, with people flowing into the central Plaza, Puerta del Sol, 'I knew almost no one when I got to the Plaza – and I met so many others who said the same thing, I arrived by myself and I just walked around and everyone was talking – all sorts of people, young, old, people from different classes, people who live in the street, all talking in groups, meeting and talking about everything.' (Conversation in 2012, Madrid.)

Similarly, in a conversation in Greece, Alex reflected on the first days in Syntagma Square: 'People who I had never seen before, people I had seen having coffee or something, but never at a protest, and they were there. They went there. It was so interesting to see and hear what people were saying even on the first day. There was even a discussion about direct democracy on the first day. But it was not organised like that, it just happened.' (Conversation in 2011, Athens.)

In Argentina, hundreds of neighbourhood assemblies emerged in the months following the rebellion, each composed of 100 to 300 participants. Inter-neighbourhood assemblies (interbarriales) of thousands of people met in parks, representing hundreds of assemblies.

'I believe that part of the impulse towards *horizontalidad* was related to an inability to trust officials', said Ezequiel, a participant in the Cid Campeador neighbourhood assembly. 'This feeling that all leaders that existed were corrupt by the mere fact of being leaders. Regardless of who held whatever formal position, inevitably he or she was corrupt, had abandoned you, and was totally separate from your problems and necessities.' (Conversation in 2003, Buenos Aires.)

And ten years later, in New York City, Matt P., an early organiser for, and participant in, Occupy Wall Street, reflected in response to a question about why so many people came into the Plaza, and used horizontal forms: 'I think we reached the point where more and more people are disillusioned with the status quo and the democratic process which represents it – and so we are trying to seek alternatives that do not reproduce this. Using horizontal forms is a part of finding ways of relating that do not reproduce these hierarchical structures.' (Conversation in 2012, New York.)

CHALLENGES AND WALKING...

The Zapatistas say, 'walking we ask questions', and they also say, 'we walk slowly since we are going far'. The walk towards autonomous creation continues in Argentina, despite the massive challenges posed by the state and by political parties. Lessons are being learned in many movements, while, in some others, the state's attempts at demobilisation have been more successful and lessons have yet to be internalised.

Sometimes the challenges that arose were foreseen by movement participants, and in these situations the groups were prepared for them. In some cases it was predicted that some of the structures of organisation might disappear or be challenged, but it was believed that this could be withstood. The argument was that the movements would continue as long as peoples' subjectivities had changed. Today, over ten years into the popular rebellion, this appears to be true. Movement participants speak of the success of the movements, and a success that is not measurable by traditional social science, but rather measured by the formation and continuation of new social relationships, new subjectivities, and a new found dignity.

This being said, there is a great deal to learn from the experiences of Argentina, as from so many other experiences that have come before us. How we maintain our horizontal relationships, struggle against the challenges, and continue to create an alternative value system – against and beyond capitalist relations – in a very grounded and concrete way, are among our most serious challenges. If we engage with it, as well as with history, I am confident that we will be able to become more than movements.

NOTE

1. The passages quoted are from the oral history I compiled, *Horizontalism: Voices of Popular Power in Argentina* (AK Press, 2006).

Part 3

New Public

This section explores the constitution of a new conception of the public in today's radical political discourse.

Owen Jones focuses on the apparent disappearance of class politics in the UK, advocating a return to the idea of class as a central political category. On this ground, he presents a set of possible and practical demands around which to articulate the struggle for equality and emancipation.

Hilary Wainwright moves from the experiences of 1968, in order to trace the fate of the 'unfinished' project of radically democratising the state. Her exploration of contemporary movements, and especially of the Occupy movement, constantly moves back and forth through contemporary history, drawing a picture of the development of radical thought in the last 50 years.

Dan Hind investigates the functioning and contradictions of one of today's most effective tools for the creation of a capitalist public: the mainstream media. Through an analysis of the functioning of contemporary media, Hind constructs a detailed 'programme for media reform'.

Zillah Eisenstein opens the discourse on the new public to issues of race and gender. By proposing 'intersectionality' as a practice of social composition, Eisenstein challenges the boundaries of social categories and explores new, possible articulations.

9

New Class Politics

Owen Jones

Class politics is alive and well in Britain: well, it certainly is among big business and their political representatives, in any case. As the playwright George Bernard Shaw once put it: 'one of the worlds is preaching a Class War, and the other vigorously practising it'. Thirty years of Thatcherism dramatically rebalanced power in favour of capital and against labour. Low taxes on big business and the rich; the dominance of the market in every sphere of life; the crippling of the trade union movement: these are some of the key elements of class war as practised by the people at the top.

This class politics has been so successful that it has even devoured its enemies. Though set up to defend the interests of working-class people, the Labour leadership capitulated to the Thatcherite onslaught long before it was returned to office in 1997. When I asked former Labour leader Neil Kinnock if the Tories were the real class warriors of British politics, his response was blunt: 'No, because they've never had to engage in a class war. Largely because we signed the peace treaty without realising they hadn't.'

Labour's retreat from class happened over a long period, but was inextricably linked to the hammering of the trade union movement in the 1980s. After the defeat of the Miners' Strike – 'if the miners can't win, then who can?', as the defeatist refrain went – the class struggle seemed to be over, as far as many on the left were concerned, whether they said it openly or not. As popular historian David Kynaston put it to me: 'It basically meant that people assumed that the old working class no longer had the power, no longer had the clout, which was a huge change in thinking.' Although identity politics became ever-more powerful – after all, history seemed to be on the same side as progressive struggles against racism and for women's liberation and gay rights – class fell by the wayside for many on the left.

Working-class politics in Britain were not just defeated by factors at home, of course. The left as a global force has been caught up by a perfect storm for the last 30 years: beginning with the rise of the New Right, and culminating in the rampant capitalist triumphalism unleashed by the end of the Cold War. In 1990, US neoconservative Midge Decter summed up the mood of the right as the Soviet empire collapsed: 'It's time to say: We've won, goodbye.' The class politics of the wealthy – or neoliberalism, as it is generally called – became so hegemonic, in large part, because a viable alternative no longer seemed possible.

The consequences have been seen vividly from the end of 2010 onwards. We have witnessed student unrest in Britain, large-scale protests across Europe, and outright revolts against the tyrannies of the Middle East. We live in a new age of revolt. But there is something bittersweet about this upsurge, because there has not been a left to capitalise on it – let alone provide leadership as, in another time, it would have done.

After so many defeats, what hope is there for the future of the left? It's worth restating the purpose of the left: the emancipation of the working class. If the left is to be reborn as a political force, it needs to build a new class politics. That means adapting both to modern political realities and to the changed nature of the British working class. By doing so, we can put the prospects of a new society organised around the interests of working people firmly back on the political agenda.

The traditional core of the left was the industrial working class. Entire working-class communities were based around the dock, the mine or the factory. Jobs were relatively secure; they were passed from generation to generation; they had prestige, and engendered a sense of pride among many workers. Levels of unionisation were high: after all, at the peak of union power in 1979, around half of all British workers were union members. The workforce was disproportionately male, though decreasingly so in postwar Britain.

But the 'new working class' is strikingly different. Miners were one of the great symbols of working-class Britain for a long time: at the peak of the industry, there were a million miners. Today, there are a million call-centre workers, surely making them as good an emblem for the modern working class as any. Or take retail: its workforce has trebled since 1980, and it is now the second biggest employer in the country. The new service sector working class is marked by much higher levels of part-time and temporary work and 'hire-and-fire' terms and conditions. The turnover of staff is high. Levels of unionisation are low: just 15 per cent in the private sector overall (compared to over half in the public sector). There remain 7 million union members in Britain today; but, as a proportion, it's about half what it was three decades ago.

So what would class politics look like in the twenty-first century? To begin with, it would look to organise in the community as well as the workplace. Where people work is still important: after all, it is what defines the working class and, on a day-to-day basis, it is what shapes working-class life. But, with people so much more likely to jump from job to job, left movements today have to establish roots in communities as well. In their own perverse way, that is exactly what the BNP have been doing: throwing themselves into community politics. From local fêtes to dealing with anti-social behaviour, from litter picking to campaigning for affordable housing, the BNP has, with varying levels of success, striven to establish a presence.

It will also mean straddling the internal divisions within the working class that widened under Thatcherism. These should not be overstated. As left-wing Labour MP John McDonnell puts it: 'There have always been different elements within the working class. The difference between skilled workers and unskilled workers; the difference between temporary workers, and all the rest of it.' But with secure jobs stripped out of many communities by the collapse of industry, unemployment – or levels of 'economic inactivity', as statisticians put it – was stubbornly high even during the boom. Those scraping by in low-paid, precarious jobs are just as likely as anyone to feel resentment against so-called 'welfare scroungers'.

Part of the problem is that unemployment has become depoliticised. The fight against it used to be one of the left's great crusades, as epitomised by the iconic Jarrow March in 1936. Fewer people were out of work in the 1970s than today, but back then it was seen as the definitive political issue of the day. Margaret Thatcher's Tories savaged James Callaghan's government with the notorious 'Labour Isn't Working' poster, when a million were out of work.

Because successive governments have manipulated unemployment figures using incapacity benefits, the terms of the debate have been changed. Unemployment becomes recast as a public health issue – and specifically about whether a sizeable chunk of claimants are *really* ill enough not to work. The argument used by both New Labour and Tory politicians to drive claimants off benefits is essentially correct: individuals and their families are, generally speaking, better off with work. But they completely neglect to answer the question: 'Where are the jobs to put unemployed people into?' Even where there are jobs available, they are often low-paid, temporary and of poor quality.

Another core demand must surely be for decent, skilled, secure, well-paid jobs. It would not just be for the sake of the unemployed. It would also provide a possible alternative for many low-paid service sector workers. 'We have been arguing for the need for a proactive industrial policy', says Eilís Lawlor from the New Economics Foundation. 'That means actually deciding that you're going to support and promote industries that would fill the "missing middle" of skilled jobs, and you would tilt them spatially towards poor areas and areas that have been affected by recessions, but also policies to target particular industries.' The fag end of the last Labour government began toying with an industrial policy – but after 13 years of collapsing manufacturing, it was nowhere near bold enough. But now, with even the Tories talking about 'rebalancing the economy' and 'Britain making things again', there is ample political space to make the case for a new industrial strategy.

The campaign for good jobs could be the catalyst for far-reaching social change. Jobs could be created to help solve the deep-seated problems affecting working-class communities. Housing is one of the biggest crises facing many working-class families: a national programme to build socially owned housing would need an army of skilled labour, as well as stimulating the construction industry and in turn creating yet more good jobs. As Defend Council Housing's Alan Walter put it in the dying days of New Labour, now that the market had failed to provide for people's needs it was time to 'invest in building a third generation of first-class council homes that are well-built and designed to the highest environmental standards, with good community facilities and transport links, and we can finally get away from housing being something you speculate on and concentrate on providing homes for the twenty-first century'.

A jobs movement could also meet the challenge posed by the environmental crisis. A 'Green New Deal' that builds a thriving renewable-energy sector and launches a national crusade to insulate homes and businesses could employ hundreds of thousands of people. As well as providing an array of new jobs, it would give working-class people a stake in the environment by transforming it into a bread-and-butter issue. This is class politics with a green tinge.

Clearly, these new jobs would not replace the old ones, and nor should they. Get rid of all the cleaners, rubbish collectors, bus drivers, supermarket checkout staff and secretaries, for example, and society will very quickly grind to a halt. On the other hand, if we woke up one morning to find that all the highly paid advertising executives, management consultants and private equity directors had disappeared, society would go on much as it did before: in a lot of cases, probably quite a bit better. So, to begin with, workers need to reclaim a sense of *pride* and social worth. Doing so would be a big step forward in making the case that the wages and conditions of low-paid jobs must be improved in order to reflect the importance they have in all of our lives.

We have seen how work in modern Britain is much more insecure than it used to be. British employers have more freedom to dispose of their workers than practically anywhere else in the western world. There is an army of temporary agency workers, lacking even basic rights, who can be dismissed at a moment's notice. As well as the feeling of insecurity that hire-and-fire conditions breed, it is thoroughly dehumanising to be treated like chattel or a mere economic resource that can thrown away as soon as it is no longer needed. There have been recent cases of workers being sacked by text message or even by megaphone. Job security must be at the heart of a new progressive movement.

But it must be about much more than wages and conditions. A new politics with class at its heart needs to address the deep-seated alienation many workers feel, particularly in the service sector, with the sheer tedium and boredom that often accompanies routine, repetitive work. It is not just about skilling up jobs and providing variation in workers' daily tasks, though that is part of it. It is also about giving workers genuine control and power in the workplace.

One of the ideas floated by the Tories before the 2010 general election was to create supposed workers' cooperatives in the public sector, offering a 'power-shift to public sector workers' and 'as big a transfer of power to working people since the sale of council house homes in the 1980s', as then-Tory Shadow Chancellor George Osborne put it. In reality, he was audaciously raiding traditional Labour language as a ruse to cover up the privatisation of large pieces of the public sector. But this rhetoric could be taken at face value, upping the ante with the response: 'Why not apply the same principle to the private sector?'

Such a call would be about bringing genuine democracy to the economy. With so many disillusioned with the ravages of the market, it would surely strike a popular chord. Instead of economic despots ruling over the British economy with nothing to keep them in check, key businesses could be taken into social ownership and democratically managed by workers – and consumers, for that matter. It would be a real alternative to the old-style, top-down, bureaucratic form of nationalisation introduced after the Second World War by Peter Mandelson's grandfather, Herbert Morrison. Working-class people would be given genuine power, instead of being mere cogs in the machine.

But a new class politics cannot simply be a British phenomenon. As the ultra-rich business elite has globalised, so too must working-class people. With multinational corporations able to hold elected governments to ransom, only the power of a strong, international labour force can meet the challenge. Only by making common cause with the burgeoning workforces of India and China can British workers hope to stem the consequences, and ultimately reverse the logic, of a global 'race-to-the-bottom' in pay and conditions.

The folly of a society organised around the interests of a wealthy elite has been exposed by an economic crisis sparked by the greed of the bankers. A new class politics would provide the basis for a challenge to the hegemonic, unchallenged class politics of the wealthy. It offers hope for the revival of a genuine socialism adapted to the realities of twenty-first-century Britain. And, above all, it would put a new society based around people's needs, rather than private profit, back on the agenda again.

10
'An Excess of Democracy'

Hilary Wainwright

The ability of the Occupy movement to create platforms outside our closed political system to force open a debate on inequality, the taboo at the heart of the financial crisis, is impressive. It is a new source of political creativity from which we all have much to learn.

At the same time, no veteran of the movements of the late 1960s and 1970s can help but be struck by similarities. There's the same strong sense of power from below that comes from the dependence of the powerful on those they dominate or exploit. There's the creative combination of personal and collective change, and the bringing together of resistance with experiments in creating alternatives here and now. There's the spurning of hierarchies and the creation of organisations that are today described as 'horizontal' or 'networked' – and that now, with the new technological tools for networking, have both more potential and more ambiguity.

And the same hoary problems reappear: informal and unaccountable leaderships; the tensions between inclusion and effectiveness. 'The Tyranny of Structurelessness', the 1970s pamphlet by Jo Freeman that tackled these unanticipated pitfalls from the perspective of the women's liberation movement in particular, may be well read.

FROM SOCIAL REBELLION TO CAPITALIST RENEWAL

The fate of the energies and aspirations of that rebellious decade involves a long and complex cluster of stories. To consider their relevance today, I want to point to the capacity of capitalism, as it searched for ways of out of stagnation, to feed opportunistically on the chaotic creativity and restless experimental culture of the movements of the 1960s and 1970s. Much of the innovative character of capitalism's renewal in the 1980s and 1990s – underpinned by the expansion of credit – came from sources external to both the corporation and the state. In fact, frequently its origins lay in resistance and the search for alternatives to both.

For example, from the 1980s, at the same time as attacking the trade unions, corporate management was also dismantling the military-style hierarchies characteristic of many leading companies and decentralising the production process. A new generation of managers, especially in the newer industries, was recognising that workers' tacit knowledge was a rich source of increased productivity and greater profits – so long as workers had little real power over their distribution.

Another example is how, in the endless search for new markets, culturally savvy marketing managers were able to identify and exploit the commercial opportunities in the expanded horizons and wants of the increasing mass of women with incomes of their own. In other words, capital proved very much more nimble in responding to – and appropriating – the new energies and aspirations stimulated by the critical movements of the 1960s and 1970s than did the parties of the left – for which these movements could have been a force for democratic renewal.

WHAT KIND OF A COUNTER-MOVEMENT?

Now, with the credit that underpinned the apparent ebullience of this particular period of capitalism having become toxic, the search for alternatives is back. As I write, the *Financial Times*, much to its own astonishment, is publishing a week of articles on 'The Crisis of Capitalism'. The opening article declares that 'at the heart of the problem is widening inequality'.

Are we seeing in the combination – not necessarily convergence – of unease within at least the cultural elites, and the growth of sustained popular resistance and public disgruntlement, the emergence of what Karl Polanyi called a 'counter-movement' to the socially destructive consequences of rampant capitalism? And to what extent might the ideas of the movements of the 1960s and 1970s influence the character of that counter-movement?

A FUNDAMENTAL BREAK

To answer this we need, briefly, to remind ourselves of the core nature of the original social critique made by the 1960s/'70s movements and in particular the nature of its potential break with the institutions of the postwar order: their paternalism, their exclusions, their narrow definition of democracy and their assumption that production and technology were value neutral.

Central to the character of this critique was its aspiration to overcome the debilitating dichotomies of the Cold War: between the individual and the collective/social; freedom and solidarity/ equality; 'free' market versus 'command' state – dichotomies that were refrozen through neoliberalism and the manner of the fall of the Berlin Wall.

The ideas and practices of the women's movement are particularly illustrative. This movement came about partly from the gender-blind inconsistencies and incompletely fulfilled promises of the radical movements of the time. It deepened and extended their innovations, adding insights arising from women's specific experiences of breaking out of their subordination.

Especially important here was an insistence on the individual as social and the collective as based on relations between individuals: a social individualism and a relational view of society and social change. After all, the momentum of the women's liberation movement was animated both by women's desire to realise themselves as individuals and their determination to end the social relationships that blocked these possibilities. This required social solidarity: an organised movement.[1]

The nature of its organisation was shaped by a constant attempt to create ways of organising that combined freedom and autonomy – what every woman struggles for in her own life – with solidarity, mutuality and values of equality. The result was ways of relating that both allowed for autonomy and also achieved coordination and mutual support, without going through a single centre. In other words, here was what could be called an early, pre-ICT, 'networked' form of organisation.

THE POLITICAL ECONOMY OF NETWORKS

This networked form was distinctive because integral to its origin, character and sustainability were values of solidarity and equality and democracy. Awareness of these origins could help us now, when networked organisations are everywhere, to distinguish between the instrumental use of the concept of network in essentially undemocratic organisations and, on the other hand, as a way of connecting distributed activities based on shared values of social justice and democratically agreed norms.

The latter possibility is radically enhanced through the new information and communications technology in its non-proprietorial forms. The new possibilities of systems coordinating a multiplicity of autonomous organisations with shared values, through democratically agreed norms or protocol, can help upscale economic organisations based on non-capitalist – collaborative, P2P, cooperative or other social and democratic – forms of ownership, production, distribution and finance.

What enables us to make this apparently surprising leap from the forms of organisation shaped by the consciousness-raising groups of the women's movement (or indeed other civil society initiatives of the same period, such as the factory shop stewards' committees combining against multi-plant, multinational corporations and developing alternative plans for socially useful production[2]) is the importance they give to practical, experiential knowledge and the need to share and socialise it.

THE POLITICAL ECONOMY OF KNOWLEDGE

The reason why this is important for the development of a political economy beyond capitalism is that behind the imposed choice between capitalist market and the state is the polarisation between scientific, social and economic knowledge on the one hand and practical knowledge on the other. While the former was regarded as the basis of economic planning and centralised through the state, defenders of the free market held up the latter as being entered into individually by the entrepreneur and capable of coordination only through the haphazard workings of the market, based on private ownership. The relevant breakthrough of the women's and other movements of the 1960s and '70s was to make the sharing and socialising of experiential knowledge – in combination with scientific forms – fundamental to their purposeful, but always experimental, organisations. And to do so through consciously coordinated/networked and self-reflexive relations between autonomous/distributed initiatives.

Translating this into economics in the age of information and communications technology – a project requiring much further work – points to the possibility of forms of coordination that can include and help to regulate a non-capitalist market. A regulated, socialised market, that is, in which the drive to accumulate and make money out of money is effectively suppressed. It also provides a basis for democratising and, where appropriate, decentralising the state, within the framework of democratically agreed social goals (such as concerning equality and ecology).

It is over these issues concerning the sharing of knowledge and information and the implications for the relationship between autonomy and social coordination that the ideas coming from the Occupy movement can creatively converge with those of earlier movements. It is interesting in this context to read the economics working group of Occupy London describing in the *Financial Times* how Friedrich Hayek, the Austrian economist and theorist of free-market capitalism, with his ideas on the significance of distributed knowledge, is 'the talk of Occupy London'. No doubt this was partly a rhetorical device for the FT audience. But the challenge of answering Hayek and his justification of the free market on the basis of a theory of distributed practical and/or experiential knowledge does provide a useful way of clarifying for ourselves the importance of the networked social justice initiatives of today and the anti-authoritarian social movements of the past for an alternative political economy.[3]

There is a point at which Hayek's critique of the 'all knowing state' at first glance converges with the critique of the social democratic state made by the libertarian/social movement left in the 1960s and '70s. Both challenge the notion of scientific knowledge as the only basis for economic organisation and both emphasise the importance of practical/experiential knowledge and its 'distributed' character. But when it comes to understanding the nature of this practical knowledge and hence its relation to forms of economic organisation, these perspectives diverge radically.

Whereas Hayek theorises this practical knowledge as inherently individual and hence points to the haphazard, unplanned and unplannable workings of the market and the price mechanism, the radicals of the 1960s/'70s took a very different view. For them, the sharing of knowledge embedded in experience and collaboration to create a common understanding and self-consciousness of their subordination and of how to resist was fundamental to the process of becoming a movement. In contrast to the individualism of Hayek, their ways of organising assumed that practical knowledge could be socialised and shared. This led to ways of organising that emphasised communication and shared values as a basis for coordination and a common direction. It provided the basis for purposeful and therefore more or less plannable action – action that was always experimental, never all-knowing; the product of distributed intelligence that could be consciously shared.

It could be argued that the movements of the 1960s and '70s applied these ideas especially to develop an – unfinished – vision of democratising the state. This took place both through attempts to create democratic, participatory ways of administering public institutions (universities and schools, for example) and through the development of non-state sources of democratic power (women's centres, police monitoring projects and so on). It involved working 'with/in and against' the state, such as when the Greater London Council was led by Ken Livingstone in the early 1980s.

Today's movements are effectively focusing their energies especially on challenging the oligarchic market, and the injustice of corporate, financial power. Here the development of networked forms are increasingly linked to distributed economic initiatives – co-ops, credit unions, open software networks, collaborative cultural projects and so on. In this way, today's movements are beginning to develop in practice a vision of socialising production and finance and creating an alternative kind of market, complementary to the earlier unfinished vision of democratic public power. A vision of an organised democratic civil society which functions as an economic actor, both in the provision of public goods and in the sphere of market exchange.

CULTURAL EQUALITY

This emphasis on the development of strategies for political and economic change that empower democratic civil society, rather than an exclusive reliance on the state, marks a distinct development beyond the politics of the social democratic reformers of the past. The architects of the welfare state and the postwar order, with all its achievements and limits, believed in economic and political reform. But they did so generally on the basis of assumptions of cultural superiority: they, the professionals, knew what was best for the masses. By contrast, the rebellions of the 1960s and '70s were asserting cultural equality. Their goals concerned economic and social needs in a context of challenging dominant understandings of knowledge, emphasising the public importance of practical, tacit and experiential knowledge. This underpinned commitment to developing organisations in the workplace and wider society that could share this knowledge and turn it into a source of transformative power.

The anti-capitalist movements since the late 1990s are remaking that struggle, in radically changed political and economic circumstances. The context is framed by a new form of cultural domination. It is in effect the imposition of a financial accounting mentality. Thus, pensioners are defined as a 'burden'; workers are defined as 'costs'. Higher education is defined as a personal investment, as if everyone determined their future in terms of a personal rate of return rather than in terms of a contribution to society. The aim is a culture of acquiescence to the cuts and privatisation in the interests of an unproblematised goal of 'growth'.

How can we challenge these new forms of cultural subordination, turning citizens, by the diktat of an imposed accounting system, into mere 'hands' or 'dependants', in the language of nineteenth-century capitalism?

ALTERNATIVE VALUES IN MATERIAL PRACTICE

Part of the answer can be found by illustrating in practice the alternative values that could found a political economy based on a framework of equality, mutuality and respect for nature. Many such illustrations are up and spreading: credit unions that organise finance as a commons; public sector workers countering privatisation with proposals for improving and democratising services for and with fellow citizens; 'free culture' networks insisting on the use of ICT as a means of extending and enriching the public sphere rather than as a digital oilfield for profit; a revival of cooperatives and collective consumer action around energy, food and other spheres in which the logic of capital is particularly destructive to society and the environment. The strategic question we have to work on is how to generalise from, interconnect and extend these scattered developments.

In this sense the insistence on 'being the change we want to see' and creating alternatives here and now has a macro significance as well as a micro one. The exhaustion of the existing system in some ways goes far deeper than in the 1960s and '70s, but we should never underestimate the ability of capital to adapt and appropriate – which is why we must think ambitiously, though remaining grounded, about our collective organisational innovations.

FINALLY, WHAT ABOUT RELATIONS WITH THE STATE?

One of the distinctive features of the recent movements and the steady development across the world of forms of social or, more radically, solidarity economics is an ambition to be part of a process of systemic change. This inevitably raises the question of the relation of these usually autonomous initiatives to the state and to electoral politics.

Most activists in these experiments, rightly, have no faith in the ability of the political class to lead the way out of the crisis. But there has been an overly generalised theorisation of engagement with political institutions as necessarily counterposed to the building of non-capitalist economic relations in whatever spaces can be struggled for now. Experience points to the possibility of a pragmatic and cautious engagement with political institutions from a consciously and determinedly autonomous base.

We could look at Argentina, where networks of workers' co-ops have struggled for legislation favourable to their interests. For example, starting with support at a municipal and provincial level in Buenos Aires, they have won the legal right to maintain ownership and control of occupied factories. The logic of their approach has been to develop autonomous sources of power rooted in actual alternatives, rather than merely forms of pressure and protest that leave the creative initiative (or rather lack of it) with the political class.[4]

This experience effectively illustrates an alternative recognition of the creative, productive power of civil society to the one described earlier in terms of capitalism's ability to absorb and subordinate the creativity of the critical culture of the 1960s and '70s.

IN CONCLUSION

This brings us back to my opening question of what use there might be in revisiting these earlier movements. In sum, my arguments point to the importance of the unfinished foundations in democratic civil society of an alternative political economy

– including a different kind of state. You could say we were rudely interrupted in our work. But maybe, as we join with new generations with capacities and visions way beyond our own, we will be collectively stronger if we recover what was potentially powerful and what the elites feared and tried to destroy.

It's not easy to sum up succinctly what the managers of the ruling order felt so threatened by in the 1960s and '70s, so let's use the words they employed themselves. It was 'an excess of democracy' that lay behind 'the reduction of authority', concluded the Trilateral Commission when it investigated the causes of the political and economic crises of the early 1970s on behalf of governments of the dominant western powers. The elite alarm at that time was thus more than just the regular ruling class fear of the mob. The notion of 'an excess of democracy' implied a fear of intelligent and organised opposition, which was thus less easy to counter.

It was the autonomous and yet purposeful, organised and capable nature of the movements – including, perhaps especially, in the workplace – that they feared most. Here was the emergence of a new generation with allies throughout society that no longer accepted the place allotted to them by the elite democracy handed down to them after the war. And yet that generation comprised the children of the postwar democratic order, gaining legitimacy through appealing to its claims and its unfulfilled promises. At that moment, the elites lost their authority. Simple repression would no longer work – not that they didn't try it.

As the ideas of the radical movements began to shape political debate in the mid 1970s and early 1980s, the threat, at least in the UK, became that a form of socialism (or at least a viable political vision threatening to the elites) might emerge that could no longer be dismissed by reference to the failure of the Soviet model. Norman Tebbit, Margaret Thatcher's right-hand hatchet man, put it neatly in reference to the radically democratic Greater London Council of the early 1980s: 'This is the modern socialism and we must destroy it.'

The grounds for these fears lay in the distinctive features of those movements and projects described in this chapter. In their ways of organising (combining autonomy and cooperation, creating the participatory conditions for the genuine sharing of knowledge), the alliances they built (across the traditional divides of economics, culture, labour and community), and their vision (beyond state versus market, individual versus social), they held out in practice the possibility of an alternative, participatory and cooperative political economy.

For a time, the new political culture seemed unstoppable. Now, in the presence of Occupy and the multiplicity of movements that share in new ways the same hopeful characteristics, it feels as if, like a mountain stream that for a while disappeared from sight, the same excess of democracy, with its springs in the 1960s and 1970s, is bubbling up again.[5]

NOTES

1. See Sheila Rowbotham, '1968: Spring-board for Women's Liberation', in Karen Dubinsky et al., *New World Coming: The Sixties and the Shaping of Global Consciousness* (Between the Lines, 2009).

2. See http://www.redpepper.org.uk/a-real-green-deal

3. See http://www.tni.org/archives/books_arguments

4. See web.gc.cuny.edu/politicalscience/faculty/pranis/pubs/WUSA_273.pdf

5. Many thanks to Marco Berlinguer, Roy Bhaskar, Jackie Cock, Robin Murray, Doreen Massey and Jane Shallice.

11

A Programme of Media Reform

Dan Hind

The aristocrats of intelligence find that there are truths which should not be told to the people. As a revolutionary socialist, and a sworn enemy of all aristocracies and all tutelage, I believe to the contrary that the people must be told everything. There is no other way to restore them to their full liberty.

Mikhail Bakunin

The mass media aren't working. And their failures undermine our claims to be the free citizens of a democracy. Tocqueville once said that in a democracy public opinion is sovereign. But if public opinion is subject to manipulation by unaccountable actors, what difference does it make that public opinion is sovereign? If we rely on a fictional account of the world when making decisions then the authors of the fiction have a better claim to be in charge than we do.

The question is what, if anything, we should do about it.

Some journalists and commentators are in the habit of insisting that their profession has learnt the error of their ways. This is, after all, what they said after the Savings and Loans crisis, after the Asian crisis, the Dot.com collapse and the accounting scandals of the early years of the century. They announced that lessons had been learned, that the profession had repented of its former dependence on sources in the state and other institutions.

Journalists told us that they would no longer succumb to the usual bribes and threats. In the period leading up to the financial crisis in 2007 they once again succumbed to the usual bribes and threats. A similar story can be told about the media's performance in other highly consequential matters; the reporting in the run-up to the invasion of Iraq, for example. The Leveson

Inquiry shouldn't distract us from this record of persistent failure. Clearly, as the saying goes, something must be done.

It is tempting perhaps to think that a mixture of new technology, citizen journalism and foundation funding will bring about the changes we need. I don't want to downplay the achievements of citizen journalism, or to deny that social network software can be extremely useful in circulating information. And direct action can be extremely effective in changing the news agenda. The most successful publishing operation of the last two years has arguably been the UK Uncut movement. They've made extensive and creative use of new technology as well as the age-old trick of turning up. In the process they have done far more than the conventional media to open up debate about tax evasion and avoidance, and hence about the deep structure of the British economy. To some extent they've driven tax into the mainstream.

But the debate has been conducted on the mainstream's terms. Cue Jeremy Paxman asking why on earth people were demonstrating against something that was perfectly legal – a point that would have been familiar to the defenders of slavery in the nineteenth century. Besides, the most significant programme of direct action in my lifetime rarely featured in the main news bulletins until those bulletins were in a position to blur the distinction between non-violent civil disobedience and the antics of those who like wearing balaclavas.

New technologies are not a substitute for the mass media, however important they might be. What we ourselves can find out is important. But what we know that others know is also often crucial. At the moment beliefs shared by very large majorities scarcely enter the circuits of widely broadcast speech. If I watch the news on one of the major networks I know that a large audience is watching with me. And reliable access to these large audiences is still the gift of a few editors in a few organisations.

As I was writing the talk on which this chapter is based I saw a tweet from someone called @StarSparkle_UK: 'I've not heard it mentioned once in British media ... How much airtime, if any have BBC given to the protests in Wisconsin?'

It's a good question. Not much is the answer. Similarly, during the student demonstrations very rich information networks sprang up among the students themselves. But mainstream coverage largely kept to its own version of what was going on. What seemed to me at any rate to be the beginnings of a wide-ranging and principled rejection of the Coalition's agenda was presented on the BBC as the usual mix of narrow self-interest and violent extremism. I suspect that the events in Britain in the Autumn of 2010 will come to seem far more significant than those of 1968, say. The occupations happened in many more universities, many more British students were involved, and the political programme outlined came much closer to the concerns of the wider population. The major media for the most part missed this and left the bulk of the population quite innocent of what was happening. And while the media certainly notices the occupations in Britain and worldwide, they retained control of the frame in which they were discussed. Viewers and listeners could be forgiven for thinking that the occupations were only an expression of moral concern. Their significance as efforts to create a culture of public communication was mostly ignored.

As for citizen journalism, for all its successes, investigations are often expensive and time-consuming – do we really imagine that we can leave the steady provision of difficult-to-find information to unpaid volunteers? UK Uncut itself began in response to an article in *Private Eye* magazine. The Wikileaks organisation originally thought that citizen volunteers would trawl through large amounts of data and find the newsworthy material. In the event they were forced to enter into a more or less unhappy partnership with the *Guardian*, the *New York Times* and *Der Spiegel*. Those who champion volunteerism in the media must remember that money will always matter in the communications industry, a point that salaried progressives often struggle to grasp.

However admirable the work of organisations like Pro Publica and the Bureau of Investigative Journalism might be, it is reckless to think that foundation funding alone will make up for deficiencies in existing investigative journalism. The foundations retain an unaccountable decision-making structure and in the past they have tended to reflect the attitudes and biases found in other powerful institutions. The result, in the words of one scholar, Donald Fischer, has been 'a culture of sophisticated conservatism'.[1]

In foundation-funded journalism, decisions about what to investigate are taken in private by people whose self-image and market value both depend on the notion that they know better than the public what the public interest is. Like conventional editors and journalists they are what Mikhail Bakunin called 'aristocrats of intelligence', and all too prone to find that 'there are truths which should not be told to the people'. The keen interest of the intelligence agencies in the internal structure of influential foundations can only make matters murkier.

The problems in mainstream provision are structural – in the sense that they are the product of existing power relations. Reform, if it is to be effective, must be structural in nature. It must aim to make the creation – and communication – of public opinion a public concern. This requires that we secure the means to generate accurate, timely and relevant information about our conditions, the means to discover what our fellow citizens make of this information, and to use existing and novel institutional forms to determine how we respond.

In order to do this I propose, as a first step, that we open up two points of decision in news production to democratic participation.

Firstly, I propose that we democratise the distribution of material support to journalists and researchers.

Secondly, I propose that we democratise decisions about the amount of prominence given to the results of particular investigations.

How would we do this? Well, in Britain we would set aside a sum of public money and distribute it to the English regions and the devolved nations. Journalists and researchers would post proposals for projects to an agreed format. Everyone interested in current affairs in a given area would be free to vote on the projects they wanted to see funded. When a project reached a certain threshold of support the funds would be released to the researchers.

The results of the investigation would be published online but they would be voted on again to determine how much prominence they were given on, say, the broadcast news.

As we know local newspapers and regional television news are struggling in the face of competition from the internet, from cable and satellite television, and so on. Public money controlled directly by the public could be used to subsidise local and regional news media – so long as the publishing agenda was open to democratic decision-making. A well-designed system would help stories initiated anywhere reach a national audience.

People wring their hands about the decline of civic journalism. This approach will strengthen local and regional news provision. But it will do so without subsidising unaccountable and demonstrably unsafe news organisations.

The money could be secured through imposing a levy on large financial institutions. They were able to lend recklessly and generate unsustainable profits over the last generation in the absence of an effectively invigilating media system. They paid considerable sums to news organisations and academics in a very successful effort to control the climate of opinion. Their critics were marginalised and journalists were made drowsy by the mantra that deregulation was good. There is a strong case for making the banks pay for a journalistic culture that will remain awake in future. After all, state supervision can only be relied on if the public understand the need for it and vocally support it.

Alternatively the money could be 'top-sliced' from the BBC. This sometimes provokes howls of outrage from the defenders of public sector broadcasting. But the BBC has also failed in recent years. It would benefit from a parallel reporting establishment that was directly beholden to the public. After all, the BBC is committed to balance. Investigative journalism is, and should be, highly unsettling. Let editors at the BBC leave the public to commission the really controversial stuff. They can then report in a balanced way on the ensuing resignations, reshuffles and general elections.

The reforms I propose would have a number of important effects.

First, they would widen the realm of civic equality, the realm in which market relations are suspended or heavily qualified. And so it would allow individuals otherwise silenced or excluded to address others on matters of common concern. The very uneven distribution of the power to describe and to deliberate constitutes an important source of distress. Social disparagement takes place through images and stories, and public commissioning would give everyone more power to challenge the claims made about them. Ethnic minorities, women, the young, and the poor should have the power to determine for themselves what kinds of information they need. They should also have the means to challenge untrue claims about themselves in a way that registers publicly.

Second, civic action in conditions of equality – the process of securing greater popular control over the climate of opinion – will make further political participation seem less daunting or pointless. The practice of debate and deliberation, and the experience of changing the field of publicity, will provide us all with an education in self-government.

Scarcity of recognition and scarcity of power incite us to a resentment that is very welcome to those who seek permanently to manage our affairs. Greater opportunities both to describe and to deliberate will help us break from the enchantments of prejudice, and to discover the common good. As Walter Karp, the great advocate of a restored Republic once wrote, 'gathered together as citizens, we recognize the citizen in each other'.

Third, and most importantly, by giving the general population the means to inquire into the nature of social arrangements, public commissioning can provide the facts, and the publicity for those facts, that constitute the only sure basis for political change. Public commissioning has the potential – if people wish to use it – to explore matters that are currently ignored or grossly distorted in mainstream coverage. It allows us to break the circuit of acceptable speech that is formed by the owners and senior managers of the major media, by the political class and by the heads of large institutions. Power currently resides to a very considerable degree in a closed structure of property and institutional relations. Those who wish to challenge that structure will have some prospect of having their views considered by a public able to act to give legislative form to its opinions.

The system of public commissioning I propose reforms the information system at its two points of maximum vulnerability. At the moment intelligent and often well-meaning but always ambitious and vulnerable individuals monopolise decisions about what gets investigated in the first place and whether the information uncovered then reaches the general field of publicity. Their decisions are opaque and even their existence is not much discussed. For all that the news agenda is presented as a simple reflection of what is happening in the world, it is in fact the collective achievement of a relatively small number of people.

To a large extent these few individuals are free to determine the common stock of things that are widely known and widely known to be widely known. I don't propose that we do away with them entirely, only that we end their monopoly on commissioning decisions.

The events in the Middle East have, I think, thrown down a challenge. The subjects of murderous autocrats are rising up and demanding freedom and democracy of the kind that we preen ourselves on enjoying in the English-speaking west. It is past time we gave substance to this formal democracy of ours, and began to discover the world as it is.

The people must be told everything. We must be told everything.

And we will only be told everything if we have the power to secure and share the knowledge we want. Absent that power we will be at the mercy of those who decide what we should and shouldn't know. We have tried that now for centuries – we have put our faith in tribunes and representatives and campaigning journalists. It is time we took on the burden ourselves. I believe we are ready.

Media reform is not a marginal matter. Journalists and editors do not want to discuss it, except in terms that leave their prerogatives intact. They are happy to apologise for past misdeeds and promise to do better in future. They are happy – keen, even – to ask how they can be more inclusive and responsive, to worry whether they have got the balance just right before concluding that, yes, they have.

Public commissioning of the kind I describe is the one thing they don't want to address. But we now have the power to make it impossible for them to maintain their silence about the substance of their power.

But first we must be clear about what we want. In what I have written here and in what I have explored in greater length in *The Return of the Public* I have tried to present this one organising insight – that the road to freedom passes through a clarified system of knowledge.[2]

It is up to us to take the first step.

NOTES

1. Donald Fischer, *Fundamental Development of the Social Sciences: Rockefeller Philanthropy and the United States Social Science Research Council* (University of Michigan Press, 1993), p. 238.
2. Dan Hind, *The Return of the Public: Democracy, Power and the Case for Media Reform* (Verso, 2012).

12

Renewing Intersectionality

Zillah Eisenstein

Because I am poised to see multiple complexities, I cannot help but wonder why there is so little news of our/US wars in Iraq, Afghanistan, Pakistan and Libya, while there is so much noise and fuss exposing the sexual lives of the very politicians who make these wars. The wars rage and people on all sides die daily and Anthony Weiner is forced to resign for sexting with young women. Wal-Mart denies 1.5 million the shared status they need in order to sue for sex discrimination, while Dominique Strauss-Kahn is charged and arrested for raping a hotel maid.

A possible explanation: Celebrity culture focuses on individuals and does not ponder their interconnectivity. At this moment in time it then becomes even more difficult to see structural systems of power and their interrelatedness. No surprise then that the US Supreme Court pretends that the women at Wal-Mart do not suffer discrimination as a sexual class because women are simply individuals who may or may not qualify for promotion or equal pay. Sex also always has a race and gender. Multiple identities exist within any moment.

What am I seeing here? What is silenced? What can I know, or what do I know here? I do know that sex is never just sex. And, sex is also always expressed with and through gender and race and class. No exposure of a sexual tale is ever simply that because sex, and with it gender, is never singly experienced.[1] Women are a sexed class (biological in some sense), and gendered (culturally constructed) along with the other multiple identities which exist – race, sexual preference, class, geographical location, etc. And this intersectional status also demands that whiteness is recognised and critiqued as a racial category of privilege although it too is constructed through the multiplicities of particular locations.

When sex is discussed as simply itself – even though sex is never 'simply' anything – it has *already* been unhinged and severed from its gendered and racial and class moorings. It is abstracted from the complexity of its intersectional roots/routes. Gender also invades the understanding of biological sex, but I will push this further fluid context aside for now.[2]

As is already pretty evident, I will be drawing broad strokes which will not seem simply obvious or self-evident. I will be asking you to connect disconnected moments and events that you might not be readily willing to do *in order for you to see newly forming intersections* that constitute women's complex lives. And I will argue that these intersecting and marbled sites are also embedded in the better known webbed status of sex, gender, race and class.

Maybe I can make my point more succinctly and then leave it to the reader to see if it works. In sum: Early forms of intersectional anti-racist feminist thought focused on the way that sexual class interconnected with race and class. Each was distinct but with overlay. Now, some four decades later I think that sexual class is understood complexly as embrocated in and with racial, economic class, sexual orientation, both inside and outside, so to speak. There is no simple unity anywhere to be found and yet shared identities exist.

All the noise that criticises sexual indiscretion – from marital unfaithfulness to rape – may appear to be in the interests of women, but actually is more about regulating and disciplining everyone – male and female alike of all colours, than caring or taking action against sexual discrimination, sexual harassment, sexual exploitation, action which would be truly in the interests of all women, no matter their differences.

I, along with most of the rest of us have become accustomed to the relentless media creation and depiction of sexual scandal, which always has a race story to tell, even if silent. The US public has been primed to expect sexual unfaithfulness in our politicians and celebrities. It is more than interesting how repetitive sexual

scandal is. The repetition is so prevalent that I do not need Gilles
Deleuze or Jacques Derrida to point it out.[3]

There is a well known line-up of these sex scandals at this
juncture. John F. Kennedy and Martin Luther King's sexual
indiscretions are easy fodder at this point in time. So are Gary
Hart and Jesse Jackson's sexual dalliances. More recently,
Republican and Democrat alike have been outed: from John
Ensign, Mark Sanford, Newt Gingrich, Arnold Schwarzenegger,
James McGreevey, Larry Craig, and Christopher Lee, to Eliot
Spitzer, Anthony Weiner, and DSK to Julian Assange of Wikileaks.
Let us also not forget the sordid and saddening publicised story
of the repeated sexual abuse and rape of children, alongside
papal denial, by priests in the Catholic Church. And, remember
to remember our sports heroes, like Tiger Woods and Koby
Bryant. And, of course there is the truly unbelievable Italian
Prime Minister Silvio Berlusconi. Most of the world is well
versed in his 'in your face' sex with young girls et al. but knows
less about his flagrant abuse of all things legal.

This list bespeaks all different sorts of sexual violation and
harassment. Prostitution is not the same thing as rape. Sexting
is not the same thing as physical sexual violation. Differing
power-filled moments constitute the meanings of sex and its
violations. Sex between consenting adults is sexual intercourse.
When sex is not agreed to, or coerced, or forced, it is rape.
Nevertheless, amidst all these differing kinds of sex, except
for in the case of the violations of Catholic priests, there
remains the sharedness of being female, and the definition of
womanhood within the hierarchies of racialised misogyny. So
there are similarities, and shared status within the differences.
The intersections that define similarity disallow an oversimplified
reductionism leading to all or nothing criteria.

Similarity means being alike and different simultaneously. This
nuanced intersection – between alike and different – bespeaks the
glue of a sexual class. Females, no matter how different they are
– individually, sexually, racially, economically, geographically,
culturally, and on and on, are also *intersectionally* similar.

I cannot help wondering if much of the exposure of sexual
scandal is more about camouflaging the war on women in

the labour force and at Planned Parenthood clinics than it is determined to remedy sexual transgressions. Given global drift, unemployment and recession, and the restructuring of the labour force, women now are a majority of the workers in the US today. These changes do not speak a new equality but rather create unsettled and unsettling racialised gender relationships that require new forms of surveillance.

Exposing sexual scandal does not necessarily change anything for the better for women. It is a form of regulating and disciplining the new excesses of sexual freedom in cyber porn and twitter-teasing.[4] With private sex being publicised, public controls are elicited. The stories are too outrageous: supposedly hiking the Appalachian Trail while really seeing his Argentinean girlfriend, the telling of repeated sexual lies in marriages, exposed bodies in cyber-land, the soliciting of prostitutes. These stories in part tell the machinations of misogyny for the powerful political elite.

My point: 'Intersectionality' as a method for seeing and thinking and acting allows for the multiplicity and complexity of the contexts that *always* define sex. As a method of thought, intersectionality pushes me to always ask about what I am *not* seeing and what I am *un*able to see; in order to try and find out what I do not already know. I use an 'intersectional' method to alert me to the multiple relations between sex, gender, class and race *and* then to take this multiple starting place and contextualise the complexity further in terms of other specified locations of power. Sexual scandal incorrectly isolates and disconnects sex from its other moorings. Women are not a homogeneous sexual class but they/we are a sexual class that is always connected with other specific and differentiating identities of power, and powerlessness as well.

Again: women do not constitute a homogeneous sex class, but they/we are definitely viewed as such, and then denied such standing because of differences within. Commonality does not require sameness. In other words women, in all their intersectional diversity and individuality, must be recognised as a sexual class across racial and economic divides, with shared interests in order to be treated with full humanity. The women in Tahrir Square and in the streets of Tunisia demanded their human rights for themselves and all Egyptians and Tunisians alike. Their female bodies spoke their sexual status while they claimed their 'poly/universal rights to occupy the public streets'.[5] They chose to not be defined simply by their sexual status, but to claim their 'intersectional' human rights with their female bodies.

I am sure that I have created some analytic chaos here. It is a chaos of the multiplicity of individuality across sexed, racial and class and gender lines. I am seeking to enlarge the issue of sexual violations in all their sordid forms – cyber rape, the sexual brutality of rape in Rwanda and Congo, the rape epidemic in US military forces, sexual molestation, sexual harassment, sexual incest, sexual torture – to their intersectional connection with women as sharing a sexual class identity within the structural hierarchies of racialised misogyny.

Female bodies in their sexed, gendered, raced context *always* intersect with their sexual class identity throughout. It is not an either/or proposition. Multiple identities require one to claim their 'bothness' as well as their other multiplicities.

Females are a sexual class despite their many many differences. Once you see this, and recognise the power-filled and emptied locations in regard to this, there is a structural, contextual meaning that begs for recognition. As such, no female is ever wholly an individual divorced from this contextual, intersectional location. Whatever the differences of sexual violation or harassment, each shares its place in a racialised misogynist differentiation of power which privileges men over women, even though each location of privilege is and must be viewed through a complex set of powerful racialised hierarchies and intersections.

In sum, and in order to begin: Sex class, and with it gender, are never homogeneous. Instead I wish to displace the idea that sex class needs any ontological status as 'oneness' and rather that today, unlike in earlier radical feminism, sex class is to be understood only in terms of the intersectional/overlapping/ multiple partialities at its core. Maybe the term sex class is not retrievable for these purposes, but I think that historical context maybe demands this change. And, given the recent sexual scandals discussed here I think that my thought resonates.

So, yes, sex class, and raced power, are multiple and heterogeneous, and their heterogeneous meanings give them their shared political import. Intersectional power systems constitute a sharedness which is not a unity, or a oneness, but rather the multiple is a kind of oneness, and there is unity in diversity as Aurobindo Ghose might say. Although feminists have written of 'diverse commonality' and 'common differences' for years, I am looking in this moment to find new articulations of the complex (intersectional) relations that are both internal and external to any understanding of race, sex, class and gender per se.

It also may be the case that women are now more diverse than they/we ever have been given newly formed economic disparities across the globe. That sex and gender and race are each made of intersections that are already embedded in them. This last point may not be perfectly clear, to me or the reader, but that is in part the point of this writing: to push to the point of what I do not quite know. I think this is a perfect commitment and methodology to be embraced by anti-racist feminist scholars and activists.

NOTES

1. This relationship has been the focus of a myriad of feminist writers for decades. For an overview and in-depth discussion of sex/gender see Zillah Eisenstein, *Sexual Decoys: Gender, Race and War in Imperial Democracy* (Zed Books, 2007), especially Chapter 1.
2. Anne Fausto Sterling, *Sexing the Body* (Basic Books, 2000).
3. Gilles Deleuze, *Difference and Repetition* (Columbia University Press, 1968); and Jacques Derrida, *Writing and Difference* (University of Chicago Press, 1978).
4. See Michel Foucault, *Society Must Be Defended* (Picador, 2003) for a classic discussion of the disciplining of sex.
5. I use the term polyversal to embrace the importance of recognising the specificities and differences that are encompassed in the notion of uni-versal. I interrogate the uni status of humanity as such, and pluralise it at its core. Poly-versal embraces diversity at the core of what unites across and through the supposed oneness of humanity. See Zillah Eisenstein, *Against Empire, Feminisms, Racism and the West* (Zed Press, 2004), pp. 197–201.

Part 4

New Social Imagination

This section explores the lines of flight along which it is possible to imagine new psychic and social landscapes.

Mark Fisher challenges the most puritanical aspects of the anti-capitalist, left-wing discourse, advocating instead the opportunity of 'embracing all the mechanisms of semio-libidinal production'. What would 'post-capitalist counterbranding' look like?

Franco Berardi Bifo unfolds the notion of the struggle against capitalism as a 'function of disentanglement'. Departing from the dichotomy between opposed powers and reasons typical of revolutionary discourse, Bifo proposes an interruption of the 'obsessional automatisms' as a powerful emancipatory strategy.

Saul Newman engages with the fundamental question of why we obey. In reflecting on alternatives to voluntary servitude, Newman claims the importance of reconsidering the 'politics of anti-politics' of anarchism and post-anarchism.

Federico Campagna focuses on the struggle of the individual against dominant abstractions. Campagna pushes anarchism out of its safer grounds and proposes a 'disrespectfully opportunist' alternative to the dichotomy capitalism/revolution.

13

Post-Capitalist Desire

Mark Fisher

Soon after the Occupy London Stock Exchange movement had begun, the novelist turned Conservative politician Louise Mensch appeared on the BBC TV programme, *Have I Got News For You?*, mocking the protesters with the claim that the occupation had led to the 'biggest ever queues at Starbucks'. The problem, Mensch insisted, was not only that the occupiers bought corporate coffee – they also used iPhones. The suggestion was clear: being anti-capitalist entails being an anarcho-primitivist. Mensch's remarks were ridiculed, not least on the programme itself, but the questions that they raise can't be so easily dismissed. If opposition to capital does not require that one maintains an anti-technological, anti-mass production stance, why – in the minds of some of its supporters, as much as in the caricatures produced by opponents such as Mensch – has anti-capitalism become exclusively identified with this organicist localism? Here we are a long way from Lenin's enthusiasm for Taylorism, or Gramsci's celebration of Fordism, or indeed from the Soviet embrace of technology in the space race. Capital has long tried to claim a monopoly on desire: we only have to remember the famous 1980s advert for Levi jeans in which a teenager was seen anxiously smuggling a pair of jeans through a Soviet border post. But the emergence of consumer electronic goods has allowed capital to conflate desire and technology so that the desire for an iPhone can now appear automatically to mean a desire for capitalism. Here we think of another advertisement, Apple's notorious '1984' commercial, which equated personal computers with the liberation from totalitarian control.

Mensch was not alone in taunting the occupiers for their consumption of chain coffee and their reliance on consumer technologies. In the London *Evening Standard*, one columnist crowed that it 'was capitalism and globalisation that produced the clothes the protesters wear, the tents they sleep in, the food they eat, the phones in their pockets and the social networks they use to organise'.[1] The kind of arguments that Mensch and fellow reactionaries made in response to Occupy were versions of those presented in Nick Land's extraordinary anti-Marxist texts of the 1990s. Land's theory-fictional provocations were guided by the assumption that desire and communism were fundamentally incompatible. It is worth the left treating these texts as something other than anti-Marxist trollbait for at least three reasons. Firstly, because they luridly expose the scale and the nature of the problems that the left now faces. Land fast forwards to his near-future, our near-past, in which capital is totally triumphant, highlighting the extent to which this victory was dependent upon the libidinal mechanics of the advertising and PR companies whose semiotic excrescences despoil former public spaces. 'Anything that passes other than by the market is steadily cross-hatched by the axiomatic of capital, holographically encrusted in the stigmatizing marks of its obsolescence. A pervasive negative advertising delibidinizes all things public, traditional, pious, charitable, authoritative, or serious, taunting them with the sleek seductiveness of the commodity.'[2] Land is surely right about this 'pervasive negative advertising' – but the question is how to combat it. Instead of the anti-capitalist 'no logo' call for a retreat from semiotic productivity, why not an embrace of all the mechanisms of semiotic-libidinal production in the name of a post-capitalist counterbranding? 'Radical chic' is not something that the left should flee from – very much to the contrary, it is something that it must embrace and cultivate. For didn't the moment of the left's failure coincide with the growing perception that 'radical' and 'chic' are incompatible? Similarly, it is time for us to reclaim and positivise sneers such as 'designer socialism' – because it is the equation of the 'designer' with 'capitalist' that has done so much to make capital appear as if it is the only possible modernity.

The second reason Land's texts are important is that they expose an uncomfortable contradiction between the radical left's official commitment to revolution, and its actual tendency towards political and formal-aesthetic conservatism. In Land's writings, a quasi-hydraulic force of desire is set against a leftist-Canutist impulse towards preserving, protecting and defending. Land's delirium of dissolution is like an inverted autonomism, in which capital assumes all the improvisational and creative vibrancy that Mario Tronti and Hardt/Negri ascribe to the proletariat/the multitude. Inevitably overwhelming all attempts by 'the human security system' to control it, capital emerges as the authentic revolutionary force, subjecting everything – including the structures of so-called reality itself – to a process of liquefaction: 'meltdown: planetary china-syndrome, dissolution of the biosphere into the technosphere, terminal speculative bubble crisis, ultravirus, and revolution stripped of all christian-socialist eschatology (down to its burn-core of crashed security)'.[3] Where is the left that can speak as confidently in the name of an alien future, that can openly celebrate, rather than mourn, the disintegration of existing socialities and territorialities?

The third reason Land's texts are worth reckoning with is because they assume a terrain that politics now operates on, or must operate on, if it is to be effective – a terrain in which technology is embedded into everyday life and the body; design and PR are ubiquitous; financial abstraction enjoys dominion over government; life and culture are subsumed into cyberspace, and data-hacking consequently assumes increasing importance. It may seem to be the case that Land, the avatar of accelerated capital, ends up amply confirming Žižek's claims about Deleuze and Guattari's work being an ideology for late capitalism's deterritorialising flows.[4] But the problem with Žižek's critique is twofold – firstly, it takes capital at its own word, discounting its own tendencies towards inertia and territorialism; and secondly, because the position from which this critique is made implicitly depends upon the desirability and the possibility of a return to Leninism/Stalinism. In the wake of the decline of the traditional workers' movement, we have too often been forced into a false choice between an ascetic-authoritarian Leninism that at least worked (in the sense that it took control of the state and limited the dominion of capital) and models of political self-organisation which have done little to challenge neoliberal hegemony. What we need to construct is what was promised but never actually delivered by the various 'cultural revolutions' of the 1960s: an effective anti-authoritarian left.

Part of what makes Deleuze and Guattari's work continue to be a major resource in the current moment is that, like the work of the Italian autonomists who inspired it and who were in turn inspired by it, it was specifically engaging with this problem. The point now isn't to defend Deleuze and Guattari per se, but to accept that the question that they raised – the relation of desire to politics in a post-Fordist context – is the crucial problem that the left now faces. The collapse of the Soviet bloc and the retreat of the workers' movement in the west wasn't only or even primarily due to failures of will or discipline. It is the very disappearance of the Fordist economy, with its concomitant 'disciplinary' structures, which means that 'we can't just carry on with the same old forms of political institution, the same modes of working class social organisation, because they no longer correspond to the actual and contemporary form of capitalism and the rising subjectivities that accompany and/or contest it'.[5] Without a doubt, the language of 'flows' and 'creativity' has an exhausted quality because of its appropriation by capitalism's 'creative industries'. Yet the proximity of some of Deleuze and Guattari's concepts to the rhetoric of late capitalism is not a mark of their failure, but of their success in gaining some purchase on the problems of political organisation under post-Fordism. The shift from Fordism to post-Fordism, or in Foucault-Deleuze's terms from disciplinary to control societies, certainly involves a change in libido – an intensification of desire for consumer goods, funded by credit – but this doesn't mean that it can be combated by an assertion of working-class discipline. Post-Fordism has seen the decomposition of the old working class – which, in the Global North at least, is no longer concentrated in manufacturing spaces, and whose forms of industrial action are consequently no longer as effective as they once were. At the same time, the libidinal attractions of consumer capitalism needed to be met with a counterlibido, not simply an anti-libidinal dampening.

This entails that politics comes to terms with the essentially inorganic nature of libido, as described by (among others) Freud, the Surrealists, Lacan, Althusser and Haraway, as well as Deleuze and Guattari. Inorganic libido is what Lacan and Land call the death drive: not a desire *for* death, for the extinction of desire in what Freud called the Nirvana principle, but an active force *of* death, defined by the tendency to deviate from any homeostatic regulation. As desiring creatures, we *ourselves* are that which disrupts organic equilibrium. The novelty of the *Anti-Oedipus* account of history is the way that it combines this account of inorganic libido with the Hegelian-Marxist notion that history has a direction. One implication of this is that it is very difficult to put this historically machined inorganic libido back in its box: if desire is a historical-machinic force, its emergence alters 'reality' itself; to suppress it would therefore involve either a massive reversal of history, or collective amnesia on a grand scale, or both.

For Land, this means that 'post-capitalism has no real meaning except an end to the engine of change'.[6] This brings us back to Mensch, and we can now see that the challenge is to imagine a post-capitalism that is commensurate with the death drive. At the moment, too much anti-capitalism seems to be about the impossible pursuit of a social system oriented towards the Nirvana principle of total quiescence – precisely the return to a mythical primitivist equilibrium which the likes of Mensch mock. But any such return to primitivism would require either an apocalypse or the imposition of authoritarian measures – how else is drive to be banished? And if primitivist equilibrium is *not* what we want, then we crucially need to articulate what it is we do want – which will mean *dis*articulating technology and desire from capital.

Given all this, it's time for us to consider once again to what extent the desire for Starbucks and iPhones really is a desire for capital. What's curious about the Starbucks phenomenon, in fact, is the way in which the condemnation of the chain uncannily echoes the stereotypical attacks on communism: Starbucks is generic, homogeneous, it crushes individuality and enterprise. At the same time, however, this kind of generic space – and evidently not the mediocre and overpriced coffee – is quite clearly at the root of Starbucks' success. Now, it begins to look as if, far from there being some inevitable fit between the desire for Starbucks and capitalism, Starbucks feeds desires which it can meet only in some provisional and unsatisfactory way. What if, in short, the desire for Starbucks is the thwarted desire for communism? For what is the 'third place' that Starbucks offers – this place that is neither home nor work – if not a degraded prefiguration of communism itself? In his provocative essay 'Utopia as Replication' – originally titled 'Wal-Mart as Utopia' – Jameson dares us to approach Wal-Mart, that emblematic object of anti-capitalist loathing,

> as a thought experiment – not, after Lenin's crude but practical fashion, as an institution faced with what (after the revolution) we can 'lop off what capitalistically mutilates this excellent apparatus', but rather as what Raymond Williams calls the emergent, as opposed to the residual – the shape of a Utopian future looming through the mist, which we must seize as an opportunity to exercise the Utopian imagination more fully, rather than an occasion for moralizing judgements or regressive nostalgia.[7]

The dialectical ambivalence that Jameson calls for in respect of Wal-Mart – 'admiration and positive judgement ... accompanied by ... absolute condemnation' – is already exhibited by the customers of Wal-Mart and Starbucks, many of whom are among the most trenchant critics of the chains, even as they habitually use them. This anti-capitalism of devout consumers is the other side of the supposed complicity with capital that Mensch sees in anti-capitalist protestors.

For Deleuze and Guattari, capitalism is defined by the way it simultaneously engenders and inhibits processes of destratification. In their famous formulation, capitalism deterritorialises and reterritorialises at the same time; there is no process of abstract decoding without a reciprocal recoding via neurotic personalisation (Oedipalisation) – hence the early twenty-first-century disjunction of massively abstract finance capital on the one hand, and Oedipalised celebrity culture on the other. Capitalism is a necessarily failed escape from feudalism, which, instead of destroying encastement, reconstitutes social stratification in the class structure. It is only given this model that Deleuze and Guattari's call to 'accelerate the process' makes sense. It does not mean accelerating any or everything in capitalism willy-nilly, in the hope that capitalism will thereby collapse. Rather, it means accelerating the processes of destratification that capitalism cannot but obstruct. One virtue of this model is that it places capital, not its adversary, on the side of resistance and control. The reactionary elements within capitalism can only conceive of urban modernity, cyberspace and the decline of the family as a fall from a mythical organic community. But can't *we* conceive of consumer capitalism's culture of ready meals, fast food outlets, anonymous hotels and disintegrating family life as dim pre-echo of precisely the social field imagined by early Soviet planners such as L. M. Sabsovich?

> Building on the whole tradition of socialist dreams of household collectivism, Sabsovich imagined the coordination of all food producing operations in order to transform raw food products into complete meals, deliverable to the population in urban cafeterias, communal dining rooms, and the workplace in ready-to-eat form by means of thermos containers. No food shopping, no cooking, no home meals, no kitchens. Similar industrialization of laundering, tailoring, repair, and even house cleaning (with electrical appliances) would allow each person a sleeping-living room, free of all maintenance cares. Russia would in fact become a vast free-of-charge hotel chain.[8]

The Soviet system could not achieve this vision, but perhaps its realisation still lies ahead of us, provided we accept that what we are fighting *for* is not a 'return' to the essentially reactionary conditions of face-to-face interaction, 'a line of racially pure peasants digging the same patch of earth for eternity',[9] or what Marx and Engels called 'the idiocy of rural life', but rather the construction of an *alternative* modernity, in which technology, mass production and impersonal systems of management are deployed as part of a refurbished public sphere. Here, public does not mean state, and the challenge is to imagine a model of public ownership beyond twentieth-century-style state centralisation. There were clues, perhaps, in the architectural marvels from the dying years of the Soviet bloc, photographed by Frédéric Chaubin: 'buildings designed at the hinge of different worlds, in which sci-fi futurism conjoins with monumentalism', 'quasi-psychedelic, crypto-Pop'.[10] While Chaubin sees these buildings as a temporary efflorescence brought about by the rotting of the Soviet system, can't we grasp them instead as relics from a yet-to-be-realised post-capitalist future in which desire and communism are joyfully reconciled? 'Neither modern nor postmodern, like free-floating dreams, they loom up on the horizon like pointers to a fourth dimension.'[11]

NOTES

1. Ian Birrell, 'Why the St Paul's Rebels Without a Clue Can't Simply Be Ignored', *Evening Standard*, 18 October 2012.

2. Nick Land, 'Machinic Desire', in *Fanged Noumena: Collected Writings 1987–2007* (Urbanomic/Sequence, 2010), pp. 341–2.

3. Nick Land, 'Meltdown', in ibid., p. 442.

4. See Slavoj Žižek, *Organs Without Bodies: Deleuze and Consequences* (Routledge, 2004).

5. Éric Alliez, in 'Deleuzian Politics? A Roundtable Discussion: Éric Alliez, Claire Colebrook, Peter Hallward, Nicholas Thoburn, Jeremy Gilbert (chair)', *New Formations* 68:1, *Deleuzian Politics?*, p. 150, http://www.lwbooks.co.uk/journals/newformations/articles/roundtble.pdf

6. Nick Land, 'Critique of Transcendental Materialism', in *Fanged Noumena*, p. 626.

7. Fredric Jameson, 'Utopia as Replication', in *Valences of the Dialectic* (Verso, 2009), p. 422.

8. Richard Stites, *Revolutionary Dreams: Utopian Vision and Experimental Life in the Russian Revolution* (Oxford University Press, 1989), p. 199.

9. Nick Land, 'Making it with Death: Remarks on Thanatos and Desiring-Production', in *Fanged Noumena*, p. 281.

10. Frédéric Chaubin, *CCCP: Cosmic Communist Constructions Photographed* (Taschen, 2010), p. 15, 9.

11. Ibid., p. 15.

14

The Transversal Function
of Disentanglement

Franco Berardi 'Bifo'

TRANSITION AND REVOLUTION

The word 'revolution' is today resonating again in the streets of
Europe, as young people's future is destroyed by the financial
dictatorship, and by the arrogance of this leading class unable
to deal with the agonies of neoliberal ideology. But the word
'revolution' is misleading. Of course when people can no longer
accept the current state of things, they look for change, for an
alternative. But 'revolution' is an old metaphor for social change,
and we should look for new metaphors if we want to figure
out a way of abandoning the decaying and dangerous world
of neoliberal capitalism that has been imposed upon us as an
unquestionable dogma.

The word 'transition', like the word 'revolution', has been
used in modern times, particularly in the twentieth century,
to conceptualise a shift which is simultaneously a temporal
succession and the replacement of a social form with an other
social form.

These concepts have always involved a rough simplification
of the process of social becoming, but in the past they were
able to sketch metaphorically what happens when a mode of
production becomes unable to semiotise and express the ongoing
transformation of social culture and of productive possibilities.

WHAT IS A SOCIAL FORM?

The Marxian concept of 'mode of production' refers to the
social relations of production between the different forces that

Marx called classes (private appropriation, salary, surplus-value, exploitation and so on). The development of the productive forces – particularly of knowledge, technology and culture – jeopardises and eventually breaks the social balance of a specific mode of production. So far, however, the extreme flexibility of capitalism has been able to absorb the disconnections, the imbalances and the dislocations provoked by technological and the cultural change.

During the twentieth century, the contingencies of political and military history (the First World War, the Great Depression, the Second World War, the decolonisation process) have triggered systemic breaks in the capitalist order, and opened the way to changes in the social organisation of labour and of wealth distribution. But the fundamentals of the capitalist mode of production have never been really at stake: the Russian Revolution of 1917 and the Chinese Revolution of 1949 marked immense transformations at the political and anthropological level, but they did not radically challenge the fundamental relation between labour and capital, as the capitalist mode of production was not really developed in those situations.

The Leninist revolution against *Das Kapital* was much more a revolution against Marx's conception of historical becoming than a revolution against capitalism, as capitalism was marginal in the Russian society of the time. The historical framework of modern revolutions (the bourgeois revolutions of the eighteenth and nineteenth centuries, and the proletarian revolutions of the twentieth) has always been conceived in terms of a succession of totalising forms. The existing form was denounced as corrupt and the ensuing social upheaval aimed at replacing the old form with a new form, corresponding to a new spirit, to a new cultural and political ideal. In this sense the social movement was the trigger for a transition from an old totality to a new totality.

But the very concept of 'form' has never been dealt with adequately. What is a social form, and how can we say that one social form is different from another? How can we say that a social form is new, original? Should we think of a social form as an external objective structure of things, or should we think of form as *Gestalt*, as a subjective perception and semiotisation of experience?

The relation between politics and society has been crucial in the definition of social form. Society has been seen as the magmatic and ever changing space where countless sub-social projects and pathways cross, interweave and concatenate. Political will as the moulding force shaping the social magma, and imposing the new form. But that perspective may change if we stop thinking that society 'has' a form, and start thinking that we perceive a Gestalt of society, that we project this Gestalt onto the social environment.

THE FAILURE OF FORCE

Modern political thought from Machiavelli to Kant to Lenin to Habermas has tried to define the relation between social magma and political will according to different strategies and conceptions. These may be simplified into two general methodologies, one based on reducing social complexity by means of political force, the other on resolving the social dynamics thanks to universally shared Reason and common economic interests.

In Machiavelli, the social magmatic process is named 'fortuna', the female unpredictability of human desires and impulses, and the construction of political forms able to control and subordinate the feminine fortune is the masculine use of strength and craftiness by the Prince. Force is the decisive tool of the political power of Absolutism, and the emergence of Enlightenment is linked with the idea that political control and the conscious shaping of social forms are based on reason and linguistic convention among social and political actors.

Kant's project of securing a peaceful coexistence among both individuals and nation-states is based on the assertion of the universal character of human Reason, the peaceful action of the market, and the conciliatory integration of economic interests. Liberal thought converges with the Enlightenment project: Adam Smith's notion of the 'invisible hand' is the systemic version of the Kantian idea of universality of Reason, as Albert Hirschman argues, citing Montesquieu: 'it is fortunate for men to be in a situation in which, though their passions may prompt them to be wicked, they have nevertheless an interest in not being so.'[1]

Unfortunately, as we have come to realise in the last century of capitalist history and imperialist expansion, interests are not always conducive to collaboration and coexistence. Rather the contrary, it seems, as interests frequently conflict and fuel passions in their turn.

This is why Lenin, the self-appointed Marxist of the twentieth century (though his version is not really consistent with Marx's vision, in my view), tried to solve the conflict of social interest by means of proletarian dictatorship, and the imposition of the supposedly progressive interest of society against the capitalist bourgeoisie.

Why did the Leninist project fail, not only in Soviet Russia, but throughout the world, after 1989? The failure of Lenin's project, in my opinion, was the failure of the strategy of reducing social complexity by means of political force. It is, in other words, the Machiavellian project that collapses with the failure of Leninist communism.

AND THE FAILURE OF REASON

But the Kantian project of perpetual peace has also failed at the end of the twentieth century, together with the Smithian view of an all-encompassing free market. In his book *Der Gespaltene Westen* (2003), Jürgen Habermas asks the question: is the present international situation still reconcilable with the Kantian project of universal peace? Habermas, whose philosophical and political theorisation has always been devoted to the search for rational conventions and a peaceful cosmopolitanism, is obliged to recognise that at the end of the last century, global capitalism and American unilateralism seemed to jeopardise the possibility of the Kantian project itself, because Force (of finance in the global economy and American unilateralism in world politics) is obliterating Reason.

In his last book, Paolo Virno criticises the basic assumption of Habermas's socio-political theory, i.e. the supposed conflict-reducing role of communication: 'Far from relieving intra-specific aggressiveness, as Habermas and other happy-go-lucky philosophers believe, language is radicalising it beyond measure.'[2] In fact, language and communication are not tools for the establishment of truth, but tools for the proliferation of conflicting prospects.

At the twilight of Modernity, both Force and Reason seem unable to reduce complexity to government. Consequently the project of Revolution exits the historical scene. The idea of revolution implies an almightiness of Will in the government of social processes, and the totalitarian undertone of revolution is an effect of this idea of almightiness. Revolution, in fact, is an act that submits the social magma to political will, and replaces the existing totality with a new totality, one which is supposed to correspond to the rational expectations of the present. Reason and Force are conjoined in revolutionary action. But both have lost the effectuality that modern thought was expecting from them.

INSURRECTION AND TENDENCY

The revolutions of the past were triggered by the effects of disruption: wars, economic crises, earthquakes generating acts of insubordination and the overthrowing of the central power. But in the present conditions, disruptions no longer act as triggers of revolution. On the contrary, as the density and speed of information becomes too high to be elaborated and subverted by a revolutionary group, the disruption tends to be morphostatic, only reinforcing the pattern which has produced the disruption itself.

We must abandon the notion of social wholeness, and adopt the idea that social becoming is not a transition from one totality to another. This is why the concept of insurrection may be useful in conceptualising the social revolts that are increasingly punctuating the agony of capitalism, replacing the concept of

Revolution. The notion of insurrection can be considered a good starting point for thinking social change in terms of becoming other, rather than in the sense of replacing one form (of totality) with another. I'm trying to imagine social morphogenesis in the context of the biological metaphor of molecular recombination, rather than in the context of astronomic revolution.

What is the meaning of the word 'insurrection'. The etymology suggests that insurrection means getting up, arising, but also deploying the inner potencies of a body.

This is why I think the concept of insurrection implies much more than upheaval, riots and insubordination, but hints at the idea that the potency of the general intellect can no longer be contained by the capitalist mode of production.

As Force and Reason have failed as principles of social change and political government, I think that we should adopt the point of view of the tendency, not the point of view of the will. Tendency is not an ideal, a utopia, it is not the projection of a rational order that force would eventually implement. Tendency is a possibility implicated in the present state of things, a possibility that cannot currently be deployed because the present paradigm of social relation (the present social Gestalt) makes such deployment impossible. I call insurrection the disentanglement of the tendential potency of the social body from the present Gestalt.

DISENTANGLEMENT

The process of disentanglement is not a process of general subversion; it is not based on the occupation of the central place of power, and the overturning of government. This may happen, sometimes, but it is not very important, as governments do not govern society, and disruptions no longer trigger the overturning of existing powers. Society has internalised power in the form of techno-linguistic automatisms and psycho-linguistic concatenations (obsessional retournels). These automatisms, these concatenations, are the morphostatic tools which consolidate power in a condition of crisis.

It is no longer a matter of consensus, of conscious rational discursive adhesion to a programme, a project, an ideology. It is simply the impossibility of seizing the central lever of the rhizomatic machine of power.

The very idea of transition (as a temporal succession of a whole constellation following the abolition of an earlier whole constellation: *Aufhebung*) becomes inconceivable, and we should conceive time as a coevolution of different coexisting temporalities.

Insurrection is the self-constitution of a temporality splitting and proliferating. Social becoming takes the form of scismogenesis, the separation and proliferation of segments bringing a different principle of generation. These segments (cultural groups, aesthetic styles, modes of production) do not look for a fight, for confrontation, they just plunder when they need to plunder, escape when they need to escape, hide when they need to hide, disguising themselves and surviving in the margins, while at certain moments occupying the central stage of the social imagination.

Scismogenetic segments aim to contaminate the social body, inducing in it a chemical recomposition. Insurrection is the point of contact between scismogenetic segments and the dominant body of society.

NOTES

1. Albert Hirschman, *The Passions and the Interests: Political Arguments For Capitalism Before Its Triumph* (Princeton University Press, 1977), Preface.
2. Paolo Virno, *E così via, all'infinito* (Bollati Boringhieri, 2010).

15
Why Do We Obey?

Saul Newman

The question, 'Why do we obey?', posed by Etienne De La Boëtie in the middle of the sixteenth century in *Discours de la servitude volontaire*, remains with us today and can still be considered the fundamental political question.[1] La Boëtie explores the subjective bond which ties us to the power that dominates us, which enthrals and seduces us, blinds us and mesmerises us. The essential lesson here is that the power cannot rely on coercion, but in reality rests on our power. Our active acquiescence to power at the same time constitutes this power. For La Boëtie, then, in order to resist the tyrant, all we need do is turn our backs on him, withdraw our active support from him and perceive, through the illusory spell that power manages to cast over us – an illusion that we participate in – his weakness and vulnerability. Servitude is a condition of our own making; it is entirely voluntary, and all it takes to untie us from this condition is the desire to no longer be subjugated, the will to be free.

This problem of voluntary servitude is the exact opposite of that raised by Hobbes a century later. Whereas for La Boëtie it is unnatural for us to be subjected to absolute power, for Hobbes it is unnatural for us to live in any other condition: the anarchy of the state of nature, for Hobbes, is an unnatural and unbearable situation. La Boëtie's problematic of self-domination thus inverts a whole tradition of political theory based on praising the sovereign. La Boëtie starts from the opposite position, which is that of the primacy of liberty, self-determination and the natural bonds of companionship, as opposed to the artificial bonds of political domination. Liberty is something which must be protected not so much against those who wish to impose their will on us, but against our own temptation to relinquish our

146

liberty, to be dazzled by authority, to barter away our liberty in return for wealth, positions, favours, and so on. What must be explained, then, is the pathological bond to power which displaces the natural desire for liberty and the free bonds that exist between people.

La Boëtie raises, I think, one of the fundamental questions for politics – and especially for radical politics – namely, why do people voluntarily relinquish their power and allow themselves to be dominated? This question inaugurates a counter-sovereign political theory, a libertarian line of investigation which is taken up by a number of thinkers. Wilhelm Reich, for instance, in his Freudo-Marxist analysis of the mass psychology of fascism, pointed to a desire for domination and authority which could not be adequately explained through the Marxist category of ideology.[2] Pierre Clastres, the anthropologist of liberty, saw the value of La Boëtie in showing us the possibility that domination is not inevitable; that voluntary servitude resulted from a misfortune of history (or pre-history), a certain fall from grace, a lapse from the condition of primitive freedom and statelessness into a society divided between dominators and the dominated. Here, man occupies the condition of the *unnameable* (neither man nor animal): so alienated is he from his natural freedom, that he freely chooses, *desires*, servitude – a desire which was entirely unknown in primitive societies.[3]

The problem of self-domination shows us that the connection between politics and subjectification must be more thoroughly investigated. To create new forms of politics – which is the fundamental theoretical task today – requires new forms of subjectivity, new modes of subjectivisation. Quite rightly, La Boëtie recognises the potential for domination in any democracy: the democratic leader, elected by the people, becomes intoxicated with his own power and teeters increasingly towards tyranny. We should remember that in ancient Greek political thought, tyranny is always the other side of democracy – one passes easily into the other. Moreover, we can see modern democracy as an instance of voluntary servitude on a mass scale. It is not so much that we participate in an illusion whereby we are deceived by elites into thinking we have a genuine say in decision-making; it is rather that democracy (along with consumerism) has encouraged a mass contentment with powerlessness.

In reflecting on alternatives to voluntary servitude, on ways of enacting and maximising the possibilities of non-domination, I think we ought to reconsider the politics of anarchism – which is a politics of anti-politics, a politics which seeks the abolition of the structures of political power and authority enshrined in the state.

What makes a reconsideration of anarchist thought essential here is that out of all the radical traditions, it is the one that is most sensitive to the dangers of political power, to the potential for authoritarianism and domination contained within any political arrangement or institution. In this sense, it is particularly wary of the bonds through which people are tied to power. That is why, unlike the Marxist-Leninists, anarchists insisted that the state must be abolished in the first stages of the revolution. If, on the other hand, state power was seized by a vanguard and used – under the 'dictatorship of the proletariat' – to revolutionise society, it will, rather than eventually 'withering away', expand and engender new class contradictions and antagonisms. To imagine, in other words, that the state was a kind of neutral mechanism that could be used as a tool of liberation if the right class controlled it, was, according to the classical anarchists of the nineteenth century, a pure fantasy that ignored the inextricable logic of state domination and the temptations and lures of political power. As Bakunin put it: 'We of course are all sincere socialists and revolutionists and still, were we to be endowed with power ... we would not be where we are now.'[4]

Instead, the focus of anarchism is on self-emancipation and autonomy, something which cannot be achieved through parliamentary democratic channels or through revolutionary vanguards, but rather through the development of alternative practices and relationships based on free association. Bakunin calls on the people to 'organize their powers apart from and against the state'.[5]

It seems that we are currently in a kind of anarchist moment politically. With the eclipse of the socialist state project, and with the terminal decline of social democracy and the devolving of the liberal democratic paradigm into a narrow politics of security, radical politics today tends to situate itself increasingly outside the state. Contemporary radical activism seems to reflect certain anarchist orientations in its emphasis on decentralised networks and direct action, rather than party leadership and representation. There is a kind of disengagement from state power, a desire to think and act beyond its structures, in the direction of greater autonomy.

However, I would like to reconsider anarchism through the problem of voluntary servitude. Doing so adds a new dimension to anarchist thought and practice (or rather produces a new problematic) as we can no longer rely on the assumption – derived from the humanism and rationalism of the Enlightenment – that the subject naturally desires freedom, or is, as those like Kropotkin and other anarchists claimed, naturally sociable and cooperative.[6]

We therefore need to deepen our analysis of the subject. Psychoanalysis makes an important contribution here by explaining our psychological dependencies on power and our identification with authoritarian figures. In Freud's study of the psychodynamics of groups, for instance, what is being investigated is really a collective subjectivisation, a form of voluntary servitude that takes place at the level of the group or mass, where the idealisation of the figure of the Leader constitutes the individual's relation to other members of the group.[7] Resistance to political authority must find strategies to counter this relation of identification/idealisation, and constitute, as Borch-Jacobsen puts it, 'something like a revolt or an uprising against the hypnotist's unjustifiable power'.[8]

Idealisation is a key, then, to understanding voluntary submission. Let us briefly follow another path here. For Max Stirner, our political domination is the result of a sort of submission to abstract ideals – or what he called 'fixed ideas' – the ideological spectres of humanism and rationalism which, while formally secular, are based on religious idealisation. God still haunts us, only in different forms – Man, Humanity, Society, the State. 'Man, your head is haunted...', declares old Max.[9]

In an argument that closely parallels La Boëtie's, Stirner shows that the state is a kind of abstraction of our own power: it exists only because we allow it to exist, because we abdicate our own power over ourselves to a 'ruling principle'. In other words, it is the idea of the state, of sovereignty, that dominates us. The state's power is in reality based on our power, and it is only because the individual has not recognised this power, because he humbles himself before an external political authority, that the state continues to exist: 'What do your laws amount to if no one obeys them?'[10]

Contrary to Marx and Engels' denunciation in *The German Ideology* of 'Saint Max's' 'idealism' on this question, Stirner actually reveals our psychic attachment to powerlessness which sustains political domination. Any critique of the state that ignores this dimension of subjective idealisation is bound to perpetuate its power. The state must first be overcome as an idea before it can be overcome in reality – or rather, these are two sides of the same coin. As Gustav Landauer pointed out, the state was a relation (with oneself and with others) rather than an institution, and 'we destroy it by contracting other relationships, by behaving differently'.[11]

This reminds us of two things. Firstly, that the release from voluntary servitude is not an individual enterprise alone, but is relational. Freedom and autonomy have to be thought of and practised associatively, in terms of one's relationship to others. As La Boëtie himself suggests, reclaiming one's power and overcoming the psychic sickness of voluntary servitude always implies a collective politics, a collective rejection of tyrannical power by the people.

Secondly, it points to a new kind of micropolitics of liberty. Here we must pay close attention to Stirner's distinction between revolution and insurrection:

> The Revolution aimed at new arrangements; insurrection leads us no longer to let ourselves be arranged, but to arrange ourselves, and sets no glittering hopes on 'institutions'. It is not a fight against the established,

since, if it prospers, the established collapses of itself; it is only a working forth of me out of the established.[12]

We can take from this that radical politics must not only be aimed at overturning established institutions like the state, but also at attacking the much more problematic relation through which the subject is enthralled to and dependent upon power. The insurrection is therefore not only against external oppression, but, more fundamentally, against the self's internalised slavery. It involves a transformation of the subject and his behaviours, acquiring, as Sorel once put it, 'the habits of liberty'.

This is no doubt a risky and difficult venture, involving a politics and life of active experimentation. The desire for genuine liberty may seem obscure to many, and its path is assailed by many lures and distractions, not least the market and the commodity, the idols to which we subordinate ourselves today and in whose charms we imagine lies our freedom. If the problem of freedom was tricky in La Boëtie's time, it is trickier still in ours. Yet, the remedy remains the same. To break the seductive spell of power, with its illusions of relative freedom and relative security, requires discipline. But perhaps we can think of this as a kind of ethical discipline that we impose on ourselves. We need to be disciplined to become undisciplined. Obedience to authority seems to come easily, indeed 'naturally', to us, as La Boëtie observed, and so the revolt against authority requires the disciplined and patient elaboration of new practices of freedom. This was something that Foucault was getting at with his notion of askesis, ethical exercises that were part of the care of the self, and which were for him indistinguishable from the practice of freedom. The aim was to invent modes of living or what Foucault called 'counter-conducts' (exploring new conducts so that we are no longer conducted), in which one is 'governed less'. For Foucault, then, 'Critique will be the art of voluntary inservitude, of reflective indocility.'[13] Foucault therefore speaks of an interrogation of the limits of our subjectivity that requires a 'patient labour giving form to our impatience for liberty'.[14] The problem of voluntary servitude can only be countered through a radical discipline of indiscipline.

NOTES

1. Etienne De La Boëtie, *Slaves by Choice* (Runnymede Books, 1988).

2. See Wilhelm Reich, *The Mass Psychology of Fascism* (Farrar, Straus and Giroux, 1980).

3. See Pierre Clastres, *Archaeology of Violence*, trans. Jeanine Herman (Semiotext(e), 1994).

4. Mikhail Bakunin, *Political Philosophy: Scientific Anarchism*, ed. G. P. Maximoff (Free Press, 1953), p. 249.

5. Ibid., p. 377.

6. See Peter Kropotkin, *Mutual Aid: A Factor of Evolution* (Dodo Press, 2007).

7. See Sigmund Freud, *Group Psychology and the Analysis of the Ego. The Standard Edition of the Complete Psychological Works of Sigmund Freud*, Vol. 18 (1920–22), trans. and ed. James Strachey (Hogarth, 1955).

8. Mikkel Borch-Jacobsen, *The Freudian Subject*, trans. Catherine Porter (Palgrave Macmillan, 1989), p. 148.

9. Max Stirner, *The Ego and Its Own*, ed. David Leopold (Cambridge University Press, 1995), p. 43.

10. Ibid., pp. 174–5.

11. Gustav Landauer, quoted in Martin Buber, *Paths in Utopia* (Syracuse University Press, 1996), p. 47.

12. Ibid., p. 279–80.

13. Michel Foucault, 'What is Critique?', in *What is Enlightenment? Eighteenth-Century Answers and Twentieth-Century Questions*, ed. James Schmidt (University of California Press, 1996), p. 386 (emphasis added).

14. See Michel Foucault, 'What is Enlightenment?', in *Ethics: Essential Works of Michel Foucault 1954–1984*, Vol. 1, ed. Paul Rabinow, trans. Robert Hurley (Penguin, 2000), p. 319.

16
Squandering

Federico Campagna

Hitherto you have believed there were tyrants.
Well, you are mistaken: there are only slaves.
When nobody obeys nobody commands.

Anselme Bellegarigue (1850)

PROMISES

Why do people work? If they are not insane, they do it for the money. And what do they need this money for? To buy freedom from work. At one and the same time, money seems to be necessary to escape from the money-obsession of the poor, and work seems to be necessary to escape from the work-obsession of the unemployed. The apparent non sequitur of these connections is the description of the logical loop in which most humans live and function in today's society. Strangely enough, the very origin of their endless tail-chasing seems to be their desire to achieve a state of freedom, that is, an escape from the loop itself.

How could the human desire for freedom turn into a self-perpetuating and enslaving mechanism? Within the contemporary landscape, the answer lies in the way capitalism manages, as it always does, to follow our requests to the letter, and to return them to us realised, if slightly modified. That slight modification, as we all know, is the tiny poison pill that turns all our 'realised' demands into even tighter chains. This is how, over the years, capitalism realised the demands for flexible work, sexual liberation, democracy and so on. Capitalism always gives us what we want, but it does so in such a way as to confirm the dark warning contained in the old saying, 'be careful what you wish for'.

In the case of our demand for freedom from work and money, the poison pill inserted by capitalism is the sublimation of our desire into a promise. The purest type of promise: that ever-lasting ideal, which always lingers and never makes itself concrete. In this sense, it is revealing the way capitalist mainstream media depict the 'good life' to which we all are called to aspire. What is life like, in a happy Hollywood film or in a celebrity magazine? For the most part, it is a life without work and without the need for money. For strange as it might seem, the promise of 'making it', in the capitalist discourse, implies an exit from the cage of capitalism. And yet, in reality, we will never be able to earn enough money to get out of work, we will never be able to work enough to get out of the obsession for money. Freedom is always just a few more office-years away, always a few more bank-account-zeros away. We will get stuck in a vicious cycle, forever chasing, forever hoping.

HOPE

Hope, a monster we have already encountered elsewhere. In religion, for example, where the belief in the promised return of the Messiah isn't but a ripped kite made out of hope. We have found it in all millenarian religions, and, above all, in the religion of revolution. Revolution, the umpteenth carrot at the end of the stick – a stick, once again, made of the same hard work and self-sacrifice invoked by the Christians as well as the capitalists. In the discourse of its decrepit churches, such as those of today's 'revolutionary socialism', revolution lingers in the air as the lightest of all promises. Like the ethereal promise of Hollywood, revolution waves in front of us a cinematic prospect of unknown pleasures. A paradise which is always just a bit further, along the rough road of revolutionary work. Just a few more marches away, a few more books away, a few more party cards away. As in the case of capitalism, it is thanks to the endless procrastination of hope that the revolutionary discourse can maintain the implausible flight of its celestial promises. Implausible, indeed, as the actual historical realisation of the revolutionary discourse is hardly more than a sequence of defeats and massacres, with the occasional blossoming of the totalitarian nightmare.

Economically, we could interpret the immaterial stock of hope prodigally distributed by capitalist and 'revolutionary' institutions as the retribution granted to their hard-working adepts. A wage which resembles that of the legendary Hasan-i Sabbah, the first grandmaster of the sect of the Assassins, who used to repay his adepts sent on dangerous missions with a generous supply of hashish. Like a drug, hope endlessly calls for more hope. As the floor of hope grows thin under the hard-working believer, more hope is needed. To the point that, as one's life nears its end, the strongest cut of hope becomes necessary: hope in the future well-being of one's family, for the worker under capitalism, and hope for the future emancipation of humanity, for the worker of revolution.

In this world of deluded workers, feeding on hope and sweating pain, it is important to identify the equation that holds together the circle work-hope-work. Its algorithm is deeply set inside the structure of a promise, that is, of the magic trick that loads present actions with an arbitrary value, to be redeemed as an investment in a hypothetical future. No rational connections are necessary between the type of action performed and the value which is supposed to derive from it. How else could we interpret the connection between senseless, humiliating, soul-destroying jobs within capitalism, and their promise of delivering a future freedom? Or, in the revolutionary discourse, between the hard-work of the 'old mole', or of the isolated, minoritarian militant, and the utterly unlikely outcome of a general uprising against crashingly superior forces?

A promise is a work of hypnotism, which stupefies and seduces, while wrapping itself as a corset around its gullible audience.

SQUANDERING

But promises don't come without their antidote. Throughout history, this antidote has proved able to dissolve not only the promises of capitalism and of revolution, but also other, more ancient, and possibly more alluring ones. Revealingly, the name of this antidote bears heavy negative connotations in today's parlance: squandering.

In southern Italy, the art of squandering has been practised diligently for centuries by individuals belonging to the aristocracy, one of the most hated yet often most refined social categories. Upon inheriting their family fortune, countless southern Italian aristocrats opposed the mephitic promises of honour, wealth and status with squandering. Despite some shallow similarities, aristocratic squandering never had anything to do with the ever-celebrated, indigenous practice of *potlatch*, where goods are distributed or even destroyed in order to show one's wealth or to reinforce one's social status within their community. Innate to the aristocratic ethic (and especially so in the periods of its decay) was a silent yet firm despising of both wealth and social norms, let alone those of status. Its reasons had more to do with the pleasure and the enjoyment of the individual and of his or her circle of friends than with any external impositions. The aristocrat's dissipation of their family wealth was at the same time part of their quest for enjoyment, and a step towards their liberation from the constraints of their social role, as reproduced by the 'due respect' which they were supposed to pay to their inheritance. Squandering was, for them, a way of breaking that promise which would otherwise have made them slaves to their role, as faceless, impersonal reproducers of the aristocratic order. After all, the 'fortune' they inherited – from the Latin *fortuna* – is etymologically associated both with material wealth and with one's fate or destiny. It is easy to see the destructive impact of squandering on the destiny of southern Italian aristocracy if one looks at the historical fate of the much more 'respectful' aristocracy of Great Britain: whereas Italy lost its traditional aristocratic class, mostly because of its active self-destruction,[1] Britain still very much maintains its aristocracy as a consistent section of its ruling class.

How could we apply the art of squandering to our current position? Unfortunately, none of us are aristocrats, and our family fortunes would hardly be enough for one day of luxurious dissipation. But our material possessions are not what we should look at. Rather, we should focus our attention on the immense, overflowing stock of hope that we have accumulated over our years of hard work, both as employees and as 'revolutionaries'. We have plenty of 'fortune' to squander there.

Like monetary wealth, hope is founded on the general acceptance of a series of social conventions which associate value measures with arbitrarily chosen, symbolic objects. In the case of hope, however, the outpouring of value is not directed at material objects – as is the case with the valorisation of the money object – but to one's actions, understood as immaterial containers of value. It is through the acceptance of the promise-system that one's actions become loaded with a certain quantity of hope: you work a certain amount of hours, and you can aspire to a certain amount of freedom from work; you militate diligently for a certain number of years and you can aspire to the quicker approach of the revolutionary utopia; and so on.

Just like money functions as a means of exchange only within a money system, the stock of hope thus acquired is not spendable outside the very system which created its originating promise in the first place. One's acquisition of hope through work can never lead to an exit from the system of the promise – that is, to its realisation and to the achievement of one's freedom – as it is bound to reproduce the same system ad infinitum. Also, as time goes by, one ends up investing too much time and energy in acquiring his or her stock of hope, for it to be lost upon the actual realisation of its originating promise. A perverse process which explains, at least in part, the seemingly absurd vocation for defeat of most contemporary revolutionary movements. What would become of the revolutionary hope of the militants, if the revolution was ever to be achieved?

DISRESPECTFUL OPPORTUNISM

This is the point in which the art of squandering becomes extremely useful. Squandering hope, like squandering money, is first of all an act of disrespect. If respect – from the Latin *respicere* – is etymologically associated with the act of 'looking back at' something, then disrespect is the act of not looking back, of looking away from something. To disrespect a promise, for the one who is offered it, thus means to avert one's eyes from the value-making spectacle of the promise's tricks. This is how, upon squandering their family fortunes, decaying aristocrats looked away from the socially constructed value of their possessions, focusing instead on the immediate use they could extract from them.

In this sense, a disrespectful attitude carries a strong opportunistic element. Opportunism, intended as privileging the seizing of opportunities available to one over one's obedience to a prescribed behaviour, is the natural attitude of an individual freed from the normative constraints of all social promises. As a promise-free individual – that is, as a true a-theist or an-archist – one is clearly inclined to perceive his or her own possibilities of action as desirable or undesirable opportunities, rather than as socially acceptable or prescribed moral duties.

Applied to our contemporary condition, such disrespectful, opportunistic behaviour reveals itself as a powerful weapon in the struggle against an all-too-real monster, whose two bodies, capitalism and revolution, conjoin in only one head, work.

In the face of capitalism's promise of granting freedom through work, today's squanderers respond with a rational understanding of work for what it really is: an almost unavoidable humiliation from which one should seize for oneself all there is to take, in view of one's own dreams, desires and necessities. Instead of falling into the dichotomy between an absolute refusal of activity under capitalism – thus reverting to an ascetic or new age pauperism – or the absolute submission to its rule – typical of the believing, career-oriented worker – the opportunist finds a northwest passage through such difficult territories. He or she might decide to act professionally for a while, if this is in his or her best interest, or even to temporarily and only formally submit to the rules of workplace hierarchy, if this helps him or her in their quest for their own aims. In their relationship to work, the opportunist banishes from his or her mind any issues of social shame and ideological inconsistency, favouring instead a cold-blooded pragmatism: what is the most useful behaviour to maintain, in order to better and more quickly achieve one's own aims, that is, one's own dreams, desires and necessities?

Since, realistically, it is hard to avoid passing through the world of work, the opportunist enters it with the attitude of the looter and the ruthlessness of the deceiver. The gift of honesty, and especially that of publicly presenting one's true aims and reasons, so often myopically invoked by many radicals, should be kept for other, more worthy spaces. For work, we should reserve all the lies we have. After all, we have long understood on our own skin how the worst possible treatment we might receive is that of being deceived and exploited: we should unleash this same type of treatment onto our worst enemies, capitalism and work. Opportunism, in this sense, has to be understood as a practical, everyday form of violence to be used against our structural enemies, with the aim of achieving a victory which is not that of an ever-fading freedom, but of an immediate state of autonomy for oneself.

We should take the material and immaterial productions of capitalism within our reach and use them ruthlessly, squandering them, taking them for a ride and dropping them as soon as their use is over. In this sense, we might find inspiration in the mass looting of the 'consumers' riots' of August 2011 in London. Despite what many pointy-headed commentators bothered saying about those events, it is most unlikely that the looters truly believed that they would be able to steal and indefinitely keep the fruits of their robberies. Rather, I think they did so with the same attitude with which an aristocrat would expropriate a horse from one of his subjects, ride it for one day and then abandon it. They looted for the hell of it, and maybe to wear those trainers or use those plasma screens just for a day, then possibly resell or dump them somewhere. Rightly so, many mainstream journalists defined those days of unrest as *anarchy*: in fact, anarchy is nothing but aristocracy for all.

It is important to note how the violent art of squandering does not contain any traces of irony. Squanderers oppose the postmodern resignation of irony – with its distance between the oppressed and the oppressor, which allows the maintenance of oppression itself among disarmed smiles – with a full penetration into the territory of their enemy: the wild entry of the pillager, not that of the tourist, the deceitful arrival of the spy, not that of the prisoner.

Squandering is an extremely serious business, which requires the concentration necessary to handle dangerous, promise-loaded goods without falling into their trap. It requires a mix of wilful ignorance – of the values and promises deployed all around us by our adversaries – and a constant furthering of one's knowledge and understanding of his or her own aims, and of those shared with one's comrades.

The same attitude functions beautifully in reference to the discourse of revolution. We should enter it like savages entering a library. Burning the books that are of no use, stealing the pages that offer us useful words, misinterpreting them if necessary. We should take the idols of past revolutionaries, lined along the walls like statues of saints, and chop off their heads: there is no better place for the head of a saint than on top of a stick. We will swear no obedience to any party-line or glorious tradition, but we will take advantage of any situation of social revolt created by wannabe revolutionaries: if there is something in it for us, then we are going to take it without signing the form or doing the salute.

In order to free ourselves from the fraudulent imperatives of revolution and from the paralysis of the endless waiting for the *parousia* – only occasionally interrupted by pathetically impotent marches, or by equally pathetic, merely self-validating assemblies – we opportunists should reject the tiresome discourse of 'changing the world'. Changing our lives would be enough of a change! What is the use of sacrificing our lives for the impossible demands of our revolutionary superego, if we, as promise-free atheists, do not believe that a celestial life awaits us after death? Furthermore, if Marx used to believe (so far mistakenly) that the proletariat attaining its own emancipation would free all humanity, we could certainly respond by stating that the individual ruthlessly attaining his or her own emancipation by all means necessary will provide all other individuals who compose humanity with an example of how to free themselves. But only, of course, if they have an active will to, as emancipation can never be given but only taken.

DESERTERS AND SLAVES

In the war waged for centuries against individual humans by the regime of work – under different names, such as capitalism, revolution, and so on – we shall play the part of the ignominious deserters, pillaging the armouries and the barracks' kitchens. If caught, we shall be quick at hiding ourselves, or adopting a disguise, or, if necessary, destroying our adversaries. Yet, never, under any circumstances, shall we try to convince anyone of the rightness of our position or, worse, try to win them over to our fight. Although we don't owe any respect to the abstract names of our adversaries or to their macabre beliefs, we still shall be able to look ourselves in the mirror, as innocent of any cruelty. Nothing, of all things, is more cruel than trying to change someone's mind or to take over his or her mental autonomy and free will. Even when faced by slaves, we shall let them be slaves: to free them would be the worst act of cruelty, and a dangerous move. It is guaranteed that freed slaves who did not free themselves through their own struggle will be the first to turn into the secret police and the prison guards of the post-revolutionary nightmare.

Wild dogs, upon meeting their tame fellows, possibly employed as guardians of their master's mansion, do not waste time laughing at them, or exchanging thoughts. They sneak around them, silently, and whenever possible, they steal their food.

NOTE

1. In fact, Italian aristocracy had already decayed long before the post Second World War laws which officially abolished titles of nobility.

Part 5

Tactics of Struggle

This chapter focuses on the new tactics of struggle that have emerged in contemporary movements worldwide, and on those which could be adopted in future struggles for emancipation.

David Graeber explores the way revolutions transform the 'common sense' of the society in which they occur, and vice versa. Especially today, argues Graeber, 'the battle over common sense is more strategically important than it has ever been before'.

Nina Power concentrates on the struggles taking place at the level of media portrayals of protest and protesters. With uncompromising passion, Power reclaims the importance of understanding today's struggles, first of all, as 'a war between the ones who say there is a war and the ones who say there isn't'.

Alberto Toscano explores the notion of reform and reformism, and its connections with the regulative ideal of social revolution. 'Is a new reformism a possible outlet of the struggles which are accompanying our long recession?'

The south London branch of the anarcho-syndicalist Solidarity Federation offers a detailed portrait of the practice and theory behind their everyday struggles. Through a process of collective writing, South London Solidarity Federation explores the reality of work, education, direct action, prefigurative politics and the meaning of solidarity.

17

Revolution at the Level of Common Sense

David Graeber

REVOLUTION

We are used to assuming that, in the seventeenth century and particularly in the eighteenth, a new force appeared in history. It is supposed to have appeared mainly in the North Atlantic world of Europe and its settler colonies (cases like Haiti, where slaves of African descent rose up and created Enlightenment-inspired constitutions are brushed aside as sideshows), and to have marked a clean break with what went before: particularly, in that it introduced the notion that the people could become an agent in history, creating more just social arrangements not – as in past revolts – by appeal to supposedly lost institutions of the past, or divine revelation, but simply because they would be better. Where nineteenth-century revolutions tended to rely on mobilisation of the urban proletariat, in the first half of the twentieth century the scene seemed to shift increasingly to 'peasant wars', at least in the most dramatic cases (starting with the Russian whites versus reds, the Mexican revolution, continuing through China, Cuba, etc.). The 1960s, however, marked the high water mark of this model, and since the '80s things appear to have been proceeding rapidly in a very different direction – though it is still not entirely clear what that is. The rise of feminism in the '70s, and then, in the '90s, of global, but decentralised and in a certain sense anti-ideological (or at least, anti-vanguardist) movements dedicated to principles of direct action, direct democracy, and prefigurative politics seem to suggest either something radically new, or, more likely, a reshuffling of elements that were always there in ways which throw into question all our most cherished assumptions about what revolutionary activity really is or ought to be.

At moments like this it becomes possible to return to the past with a different eye and consider the possibility that our familiar terminology was always blinding us to much of what was really important. Were the revolutions that have become part of the canon – starting maybe with the English, but definitely with the American and French Revolutions – really that unique and historically unprecedented? Did they truly succeed, or fail, in the ways we thought?

For my own part, I've found the most useful starting place in this process of rethinking to be Immanuel Wallerstein's reflections on revolution, and particularly the French Revolution, as world historical events. It seems to have originally been formulated in response to an argument that revolutions might not have been as historically important as we imagine: since a country like, say, Denmark, might well be shown to have changed as much or more between 1750 and 1850 than France, even though it witnessed nothing remotely like the French Revolution. Wallerstein's reply: perhaps so, but would Denmark have changed had the French Revolution never taken place? Is it not better to see every major revolution as a world revolution, regardless of where street battles and changes of regime happen to have taken place? The French Revolution of 1789 redounded throughout the capitalist world-system of the time, and changed people's basic conceptions of what politics was about anywhere.

Wallerstein argues that the French Revolution was the real foundational event, however, since it introduced three basic principles that, he notes, would have been considered pretty much lunatic fringe by most educated Europeans in 1750, but to which just about everyone had to at least pay lip service a century later. These are:

1) that social change is not something intrinsically objectionable, but normal and desirable;
2) that the proper institution to manage the course of social change is the state;

3) that states receive their legitimacy from an entity that can be referred to as 'the people'.

It is only in very recent years, he argues, that any of these principles have been seriously challenged.

What I find particularly striking about Wallerstein's argument is not just the global scale of revolutions, or even what its principles are, but the notion that revolutions transform what might be called political common sense: our most basic assumptions about what politics is, how it is conducted, and what its stakes and purposes are.

COMMON SENSE

It strikes me that we are at an historical moment when the battle over common sense is more strategically important than it has ever been before. There is a very simple reason for this: it has become capital's preferred domain of struggle. This, it seems to me, is the real dirty secret of neoliberalism. Neoliberalism represents itself as a matter of putting economic considerations above all others; above questions of justice, equity, rights, political ideologies, or even law or elementary morality. In fact it's anything but. One can see this best by examining its results. As David Harvey among others have noted, the period of state-directed, 'developmental' or welfare-state capitalism of the 1950s and '60s, simply in terms of economic indicators, actually saw about twice the levels of overall growth. In other words, even by what it claims to be its own standards, neoliberalism has proved a colossal failure. Why then do elites endlessly persist in demanding ever-more extreme versions of the same thing (privatisation, marketisation, precarious labour, destruction of social guarantees) every time their prescriptions produce an economic crisis? The most plausible answer is that economic efficiency is not really what's most important for them. Neoliberalism makes much better sense, in fact, if read as a political movement, one which systematically prioritises the political imperative of trying to make capitalism seem the only viable economic system over the economic imperative of actually trying to create a viable capitalism. It's hard to think of any other way to explain, for instance, the rationale behind such ostensibly economic matters as labour policy. Creating precarious conditions for powers on all levels is not, in fact, a particularly efficient way to organise labour. But it's a superb way of depoliticising labour. The same is true of constantly increasing working hours. In fact, the same can be said, even more perhaps, of what many consider the very defining feature of the new, post-'70s dispensation: getting rid of the old Keynesian deal where increases of productivity were rewarded with increased wages, and substituting, instead, the constant extension of credit. As the crash of 2008 showed, it proved a disastrous way of organising a world market system, but it was startlingly successful in ensuring that millions of working-class people had to teach themselves to put aside any thought of solidarity with other workers, or indeed anyone but their closest family, and to begin to imagine themselves increasingly as entrepreneurs.

The cost of this emphasis on the political has – to capitalism, certainly, and also to the world – been almost unimaginable. But it has created a bizarre paradox. The current system is sinking under the weight of the apparatus of securitisation and the strange, inefficient economic choices that it has made to make itself seem the only possible viable system. But the war for the imagination is the only one the capitalists seem to have definitively won. Even when the system completely discredited itself, in 2008, no one seemed to have the slightest idea what an alternative would even look like.

The battle over common sense assumptions, at this moment, takes on an unusually strategic significance.

I should clarify first of all that I am not assuming, as many do, that 'common sense' is always, necessarily, a mere ideological construct, a way of naturalising forms of arbitrary power. To the contrary. Much of what we call common sense is the simply practical wisdom that most academic critics notoriously lack.

Yet especially when we talk of political common sense, we are dealing with something that's already a battleground, in which utterly contradictory assumptions are always at play. Often these are the sediments of very long political struggles.

DEMOCRACY

The alter-globalisation movement, originally inspired by the Zapatistas, focused largely on popular conceptions of democracy. It was in many ways an obvious choice, but not an inevitable one. Just to give a sense of how conflicted the term is: the Zapatistas might have embraced the word 'democracy', but other indigenous-based groups (Aymara movements in Bolivia for example) viewed it as a violent, alien means of opposition. Similarly, while global justice activists in the US reacted to the US government's incessant invocation of 'democracy' by trying to reclaim the term, starting with an effort to reinvent new forms of grass-roots democratic process, most academic leftists – in so far as they considered the term at all – were more interested in attacking the entire concept of democracy as an ideological construct.

Here existing common sense was not as inhospitable a ground as it would have been with terms like 'communism', 'socialism', or even, say, 'freedom'. Above all this was true in places like the United States. When one invokes the word 'democracy' in the US, one is necessarily evoking a long history of struggle, debates and outright violence, which has never been completely resolved. As a result the word remains a battleground. Most Americans, for example, are startled when told that neither the Declaration of Independence nor the Constitution say anything about the US being a democracy – most of the founding fathers were quite explicit in saying they felt democracy was the worst form of government, and that the Republican system they had created was meant to guard against any danger of democracy breaking out. At that time 'democracy' meant what we'd now call 'direct democracy', Athenian style communal self-organisation, and was used largely as it had been in the middle ages, as a term of abuse.

In fact it was deployed in much the way 'anarchy' is today – a chaotic, violent free-for-all. It was only when politicians realised, starting in the 1820s and '30s, that the majority of ordinary citizens took quite a different view, that they began embracing the term in order to win elections. So it has remained since. Most Americans, when they hear the word, continue to think of it referring primarily to individual freedoms and collective self-organisation (in much the way anarchists themselves see 'anarchy'), yet at the same time, in the official discourse, endless appeals to 'democracy' as the ultimate political value have come increasingly to refer to authoritarian versions of the very system originally created after the Revolution to ensure that any signs of collective self-organisation be nipped in the bud.

At least since the Port Huron statement, the US left recognised what the challenge really was here: how to promulgate an alternative, participatory conception of democratic self-organisation? The results can only be described as mixed. In some ways, these efforts have been spectacularly successful: activists – particularly those working in the more radical feminist, anarchist and direct-action traditions – have gradually developed genuinely effective new forms of directly democratic process, ones that have not only proved eminently practical, but also allow activists a glimpse of what life in a truly democratic society might be like. Anyone who has experienced this form of organisation directly tends to come away transformed. The problem is that it has proved well-nigh impossible to convey that sense of excitement beyond the charmed circle of the activist community itself. As a result, all this work has had virtually no effect on common sense. Most American liberals who are not activists, being basically elitists, continue to think of direct democracy as the Founders did, associating it with the frightening prospect of mass plebiscites, lynching and mob rule; while most working-class Americans fall back on at least some of the tenets of market populism, if only for lack of anything else. The best that can be said is that should a widespread popular movement materialise, the infrastructure is in place to take it in a genuinely democratic direction.

WORK

Perhaps the toughest nut to crack, however, is not democracy, but revolves around the morality of work. Despite occasional 'anti-work' effusions in the '60s and '70s, one of the few premises that everyone in mainstream political discourse seems obliged to accept is that submitting to labour discipline is virtuous and good, that anyone who does not work as hard as they possibly can is inherently undeserving and immoral, and that the solution to any economic crisis, or even problem, is always that people should work more and harder than they do already. This is a moral position, not an economic one, since it is maintained even in circumstances where any level-headed assessment would conclude that what's really needed is not more work, but less. And this is true even if we don't take into account ecological concerns – that is, the fact that the current pace of the global work machine is rapidly rendering the planet uninhabitable.

Yet it is an extraordinarily difficult position to challenge. Part of the reason is the history of workers' movements themselves. In the early decades of the twentieth century, the chief distinction between socialist and anarchist unions was that the former always tended to demand higher wages, the latter, less hours. The socialist leadership embraced the consumer paradise offered by their bourgeois enemies; yet they wished to manage the productive system themselves; anarchists, in contrast, wanted time in which to live, to pursue forms of value of which the capitalists could not even dream. Yet where did the revolutions happen? As we all know from the great Marx-Bakunin controversy, it was the anarchist constituencies – in the sense of those who rejected consumer values, who were not particularly interested in what might be termed the productivist bargain – that actually rose up, whether in Spain, Russia, China, Nicaragua, or for that matter, Algeria or Mozambique. Yet in every case they ended up under the administration of socialist bureaucrats who embraced that ethos of productivism, that dream of consumer utopia, even though this was the last thing they were ever going to be able to provide. The irony became that the principal social benefit the Soviet Union and similar regimes were actually able to provide – more time, since work discipline becomes a completely different thing when one effectively cannot be fired from one's job – was precisely the one they couldn't acknowledge; it had to be referred to as 'the problem of absenteeism' standing in the way of an impossible future full of shoes and consumer electronics. But if you think about it, even in the west, it's not entirely different. Trade unionists, too, feel obliged to adopt bourgeois terms – in which productivity and labour discipline are absolute values – and act as if the freedom to lounge about on construction sites is not a hard-won right but actually a problem. Granted, it would be much better to simply work four hours a day than do four hours worth of work in eight, but surely this is better than nothing. The world needs less work.

I should emphasise: this is not to say that there are not plenty of working-class people who are justly proud of what they make and do, just that it is the perversity of capitalism (state capitalism included) that this very desire is used against us, and we know it. As a result, it has long been the fatal paradox of working-class life that despite working-class people and sensibilities being the source of almost everything of redeeming value in modern life – from shish kebab to rock'n'roll to public libraries and stand-up comedy – they are so precisely when they're *not* working, in that domain that capitalist apologists obnoxiously write off as 'consumption'. Which allows the remarkably uncreative administrative classes (and I count capitalists among these) to dismiss all this creativity, before taking possession of it and marketing it as if it were their own invention.

Yet in the process, the pretty-bourgeois ethos of work as moral in itself – or, more specifically, of work discipline as morality – has extended from its would-be representatives to the working class itself; so much so that it's become almost impossible to present arguments against it in any forum. Finding a way to do so would seem the most urgent, but also most difficult, political dilemma of our times.

COMMUNISM

Something strange happened in the 1980s. This was perhaps the first period in history when capitalists actually began calling themselves that – the *New York Times*, which at the time became the real ideological driving force for the popularisation of what was to become conventional neoliberal wisdom, led the way, with an endless series of headlines crowing over how some Communist Regime, or socialist party, or cooperative enterprise, or other ostensibly left-wing institution, had been forced, by sheer expedience, to embrace one or another element of 'capitalism'. It was tied to the endlessly repeated mantra of 'communism just doesn't work' – but it also represented a kind of ideological back-flip, one first pioneered by right-wing lunatic fringe figures like Ayn Rand, where 'capitalism' and 'socialism' were essentially made to change places. Where once capitalism had been the tawdry reality, and socialism the unrealised ideal, now it was the other way around. After 1989, the meaning of 'communism' seemed to shift to 'whatever system of organisation prevailed under "communist" regimes'. This, in turn, was followed by a genuinely peculiar rhetorical shift, whereby such regimes – once written off as ruthlessly efficient in the maintenance of armies and secret police, but woefully inept at the production of consumer pleasures – were treated as themselves utopian, that is, as so completely defying the basic realities of human nature (as revealed by economics) that they simply 'didn't work' at all, that they were, in effect, impossible – a truly remarkable conclusion when speaking, say, of the USSR, which for 70 years controlled a quite large share of the earth's surface, defeated Hitler, and launched the first satellite, and then human, into outer space. It was as if the collapse of the Soviet Union was taken to prove that it could never have existed in the first place!

The irony is that, if one takes a more realistic definition of the term 'communism', exactly the opposite has been proved to be true. It could well be argued that we're in precisely the reverse of the situation so widely touted in the 1980s. Capitalism has been forced, in a thousand ways in a thousand places, to fall back on communism, precisely because it's the only thing that works.

All it requires is to stop imagining 'communism' as the absence of private property arrangements and go back to Louis Blanc's original definition: 'from each according to their abilities, to each according to their needs'. If any social arrangement grounded and operating on such a principle can be described as 'communism', all of our most fundamental understandings of social reality completely change. It quickly becomes apparent that communism – at least in its most attenuated form – is the basis of all amicable social relations. We are all communists with those we love and trust the most; yet no one behaves communistically in all circumstances with everyone, or, presumably, ever has or will. Above all, work tends to be organised on communistic grounds, since in practical situations of cooperation, and especially when the need is immediate and pressing, the only way to solve a problem is to identify who has what abilities to get them what they need. Hence, it's not a matter of imagining some ideal future 'communism' – all societies are communistic at base, including in at least many of their basic modes of operation, and in all workplaces; capitalism, therefore, is best viewed as a bad way of organising communism. (It is bad among other things because it tends to encourage extremely authoritarian forms of communism at the workplace level. One key political question is: What better way of organising communism can we find that will encourage more democratic forms? Or even better, that eliminates our contemporary institution of the 'workplace' entirely.)

Just putting things this way seems quite startling, but it's really very commonsensical if one starts with the classic definition of communism, and pushes away the endless ideological accretions it has taken on, both from those who claimed to speak in its name, and those who claimed to revile it. There is no reason it could not be part of everyday common sense and one could well imagine a point in the future where it would become so. But if we were even capable of framing the issue in the present day, it would be perfectly obvious what the current right-wing adoption of communitarianism, volunteerism, and the like actually means. The Tory conception of the 'big society' is only the most dramatic case in point. What they are basically acknowledging is that capitalism is no longer sustainable in and of itself. For most projects directly involving the common good, it is forced to fall back on communism, because communism is the only thing that works.

18

Winning the Media War:
Why There is no Such Thing
as a Bad Protester

Nina Power

There is a war between the ones who say there is a war and the ones who say there isn't. Those who think there is no war, who transmute their feelings of comfort and content into a universal principle, rather than reflecting on the many forms of violence that are necessary in order for a small minority to feel protected from the rest of the world, psychologically and geographically, deliberately have no explanation for revolt, protest, insurrection, 'riot'. As evidenced by much of the conservative-centrist-liberal response to the unrest in London and other parts of England in August 2011, there can structurally be no war – class war, war against particular groups of people, war against the future in the name of the elite – because to think in terms of the category of war is already to admit that one has a side, one must take sides, even or especially against the very situation in which you happen to live. Even if your country is officially at war, when even the state admits it – with Afghanistan, Iraq, Libya and a potential infinite array of new enemies – these are not 'real' wars because they come no nearer than television, the death of others, 'your' soldiers, 'their' soldiers and civilians, in distant lands and, in opposition, mass protests which after all 'failed'. For those who believe that there is no war, there can be little explanation for protest, or for unrest, or for anger.

The simultaneous demand for 'something to happen, now', and the concomitant complaint that 'nothing is happening' is predicated on an impossible demand for there to be action carried out by others, but on terms dictated by those who won't act themselves. Those who, from a liberal point of view, are supposed to be angry in order to give the comfortable the reassurance of the spectacle – students, those routinely harassed by the police, those who are dispossessed, the unemployed, the precarious – are punished doubly when they turn out to do the very thing they were supposed to be doing all along – protesting, taking the streets, destroying political and commercial property. The apathetic student suddenly becomes the mindless thug, who, even when he or she is on the street for an extremely explicit set of reasons – in Britain, for example, to protect the EMA, to protest against historically unprecedented fee increases, to demonstrate anger against cuts to educational institutions, to protect certain subjects (arts, humanities and social sciences, which in Britain lost 100% of their funding in 2011) – the 'lazy' student becomes in a matter of seconds the 'violent' student, a fear backed up and reiterated by the sentences handed down to a carefully selected few: 32 months for throwing a fire extinguisher that injured no one, 12 months for throwing two balsa wood sticks that injured no one, 16 months for sitting on the bonnet of a moving car and perhaps chucking a rubbish bin: 'Crimes' as absurd as their punishment. But their symbolic value is of extreme worth: they give a 'criminal' (indifferently working-class or upper-class, but always young, and primarily male) face to a set of rational demands, and undermine protest, which is always 'ruined by a few' and thus carefully and strategically written-off in total, as it was always going to be. The demands themselves are lost, deemed meaningless in the face of such 'thuggery'. Others who would be tempted to come out on to the streets to protest are put off, because the punishments for doing nothing, anything, are so absurd. Those with children are scared, reasonably, that the violence they see on television, even though the voice-over will claim over and over again that it is coming from the crowd, will evidently be coming instead from the heavily armed and protected police, aided by their horses and dogs.

The unrest in various British cities during August 2011 – London, Bristol, Manchester, Birmingham and elsewhere – has further upset those who yearn for something to happen but are terrified when it actually does. 'This is not what we meant!', they wail, 'these people don't have any real demands!' 'Mere criminals, not protesters!', 'more police now, more guns, more punishment!' Media is careful not to upset those who are easily frightened: between the big other (posited collective disapproval) and the little other (the disapproval of those you know) lies a more disturbing and prevalent fantasy regarding who should not be made upset, who should be coaxed into agreement, the one who is, in the end, all important. We could call this the 'medium-sized liberal other', the one who is always invoked whenever one's argument is deemed to be correct 'up to a point', but beyond that, off-putting, dangerous, will lose support. The 'medium-sized liberal other' is, however, never the exact person telling you to 'be careful', to 'reign in' your arguments, it's always someone else a bit like them, projected into some hypothetical realm – not least because, like the big other, the 'medium-sized liberal other' does not exist, except in the minds of those who won't admit their own terror at holding a position. One must be eternally worried about the mind of the person whose mind is not yet made up, one must tread carefully around the being of the eternally sceptical, trying to reassure a floating voter in a stagnant pool: he or she may – yet, in the future – make all the difference!

Is this then the 'media war' we must win? To convince the projected uncertain one that one interpretation of events and context is the correct one? To convince those who believe there is no war that in fact there is a series of multiple wars being waged that depend precisely on someone (or many someones) believing that there are no wars, and that when 'violence' happens it is absolutely incomprehensible, lacks explanation, is the product of transcendent forces that belong to the natural categories of hell – criminality, recidivism, the 'animal within man'? Our decision must be exactly that, no more pandering to the wavering: Fuck the medium-sized liberal, the one who takes half a minute to start calling for more police, more guns, curfews and jail for everyone who terrifies them. Fear is the natural medium of the elites, and property the currency: give a man a house, or at least make him think it's his even though the bank owns it, and he'll be your unthinking lap-dog, terrified of those without property, without work, without a future (however small the future of the lap-dog is by comparison). Those who protest cannot have reasons, have no 'right' to protest, lack demands (even though those who have demands, like the students, also paradoxically lack them the moment they become 'violent', and will always lack them, somehow, except perhaps retroactively, in 20 years time when they will have been proved 'right', at the moment when it no longer matters).

And after all, if we defend 'the right to protest', a defensive formulation anyway, the medium-sized liberal will always respond, with perfect debating-society logic: 'but what about the fascist "right to protest"? Will you defend her "right"? If not you are no better than she is!' The medium-sized liberal has no feeling for context, is a strange nihilist of history – but this is not enough: why are protesters 'good' protesters, and why are other people not counted as protesters at all? The answer is quite simple: fascists are not protesters. The wail will go up – 'but they are protesting all kinds of things! They hate immigration! They hate Islam! They hate multiculturalism!' But anyone who campaigns for the unequal and the promotion of inequality is not protesting anything: inequality is the current state of things, racism is the current order, Islamophobia is the guiding theme of the foreign and internal security policy of the UK, the US and elsewhere. Fascists project and articulate in simple terms the status quo, and pretend that they are the only ones saying it, hence the logic of the 'well, I know we're not allowed to say this, but' or 'I'm not a racist, but', even though the dominant culture will precisely allow you to say all of these things and more – is there anything more pathetic than the 'controversial' mainstream media columnist saying something 'beyond the pale', against the apparent weight of projected politically correct disapproval: 'no one listens to what I have to say!' whines the person who is read by half a million people.

There is no liberal vacuum in which protest is the natural, neutral, authorised outlet for a projected set of abstract complaints. When the English Defence League march through areas where many Muslims live, this is not a hypothetical action against a hypothetical group of people living in a hypothetical area. Liberal sentiment, the kind that would raise the 'but, but, what about "their" right to protest' complaint, abhors the empirical and worships the abstract in precise proportion to when either would be of use, thus 'there is nothing to explain!' about recent insurrection, yet 'I will go to the death for your right to say the indefensible' or some such liberal folderol.

If we admit there is a war, then there is no way we cannot take sides. The fascists are on the other side and we do not have to allow them the freedom to speak and protest (the mainstream already gives them too much time and space, filling news and discussion programmes with self-declared racists and fascists, dragged political discussion ever right-ward, as 'respectable' parties use their presence as an excuse to usher in yet more punitive immigration legislation or wring their hands over the 'failure' of multiculturalism, or cultures they disapprove of). It may be possible to chisel away at the mainstream media, to get a useful argument in there, some analysis in here, but the liberal medium other will always demand 'balance', even when the scales are so clearly broken. The 'leftist' is reduced to a series of characterisations, forced to jerk about like a puppet, making familiar noises – the producer will always know beforehand what you will say before you even say it. The alternative? To fight the war on multiple fronts: not to fall into the trap of thinking that the mainstream media is the only route, and that when you're there you'll be able to do something different – you won't. If your real work and thinking takes place elsewhere – in campaigns, political action, writing on blogs or elsewhere – then this is the battleground where wars will be fought and won. The media may love, encourage and work hard to create a frightened public, but sooner or later explanations will be demanded – authoritarianism requires daily work, upping the dosage so that the intolerable starts to seem like normality – but nothing can or will replace analysis, contextualisation, history, an alternative model that doesn't run on fear. It takes many years to break the spirit of a people, to destroy social bonds. We may be on the back foot, having to reconfigure our energy from defensive positions, defending those accused, jailed and pilloried, but such work only clarifies our position, makes clearer where the enemy lies, his weaknesses, and ultimately, how and when he can be destroyed.

19

Reforming the Unreformable

Alberto Toscano

For some years now, advocates of a pragmatic, sensible left have staked their entitlement to alternate in the administration of the status quo on the abandonment of any lingering attachment to the lost object of revolution. As everybody knows, with political maturity comes mourning, a reconciliation with reality, fallibility and finitude, the relinquishing of a debilitating melancholy. This familiar pattern, repeated across post- and counter-revolutionary times, weaves together a rhetoric of gradual improvement with a nervous allergy to upheavals.

Yet the present moment is perhaps unique in the ubiquity of what we could justifiably term a melancholy of reform. The economic crisis has predictably morphed into an opportunity for the reiteration, intensification and entrenchment of the selfsame dynamics that occasioned it in the first place. Residual regions of non-commodified social life are again primed for stripping and colonisation. In this context, the postwar Euro-Atlantic compact between big labour, big capital and big government has become an imaginary focal point for those still wedded, however nebulously, to the notion of social emancipation.

The pining for the Golden Thirty – 'when we still used to make things', when working classes formed communities, when even ardent capitalists recognised the notion that some domains of social life are *a priori* unmarketable – can readily be registered in popular culture and radical thought alike, as well as in incoherent ideological constructs like Red Toryism or Blue Labour. When the corrosive criticisms and energetic struggles to which Fordism and the welfare state were subject from the left aren't simply neglected, they are viewed as culprits of an ebbing of progressivism, irresponsible pretexts for capitalist revanchism. Works whose ideological compass is set by postwar social democracy are likely to chastise 'the sixties' for making excessive demands and thus spoiling a good thing through a petulant inflation in needs and demands.

Whatever the historical judgement on the causalities and limits of really-existing social democracy, it is evident that current struggles against 'austerity' (a thin Puritan mask for accumulation by dispossession), draw their impetus from the immediate need to defend elements of that postwar compromise. In particular, these struggles at the point of reproduction – in schools and universities, hospitals and public transport, around benefits and pensions – revive a deeply felt common sense regarding social rights, one that often relies on that virtuous dialectic between labour and citizenship which long informed a dominant strain of progressive opinion. Education as a public good, universal free health provision at the point of use, the 'right to work' – so many demands which, having germinated in the workers' movements of the nineteenth century, attained, in the wake of postwar reconstruction, an unprecedented actuality in certain privileged and conflicted loci of capital accumulation.

Is a new reformism a possible outlet of the struggles which are accompanying our long recession? In its principal twentieth-century form, reformism retained for a long time its connection to the regulative ideal of social revolution. Fundamental transformation was to mature gradually, even imperceptibly, out of the socialising tendencies inherent to modern capitalism, channelled and checked by organised labour and its parties. Such a philosophy of history and action fared much better in some economic conjunctures than others. Until ruling-class strategies and organic crisis undermined it, the curve of capitalist accumulation could plausibly resemble a cumulative movement towards emancipation.

Ever since the last, thwarted burst of genuine reformism, in the guise of the socialisation measures proposed by Rudolf Meidner in Sweden, the very notion of reform has been fundamentally evacuated of meaning or irrevocably traduced. With the mutation of social democracy into social liberalism, reform has come to mean either the rollback of the outcomes of social democracy, in ominous expressions such as 'pension reform', or the (rarer) proposal of initiatives to alleviate inequality or offset the more parlous effects of the profit motive, without, needless to say, in any way questioning it. Whereas the reformism born of the Second International was comforted by a teleology at once economic and ethical, those who may present themselves as reformist today are advocates not so much of a *telos* as a *katechon* – the Biblical notion, revived by Carl Schmitt, of that brake which restrains the Antichrist's dominion over the Earth. Whether to prevent its degeneration into barbarism or the bursting apart of its integument, or both, capital is to be embedded, fettered, civilised, made 'socially responsible'.

Though it could be argued that high Keynesian reformism also didn't fundamentally intervene on the basic parameters of capital as a social relation, the 'reformism' of today's social liberals is immeasurably more cosmetic. Indeed, as we are reminded on a daily basis, it can only present itself as a benevolent political manager of accumulation on the upswing of the business cycle, and descends into impotent pantomime as soon as it is faced with a crisis.

This reformism without reforms can be contrasted with the proliferation of prescriptions for reform shorn of reformism; measures, be they political or economic, that propose radical alterations of current relations of power and production, without heralding a fundamental upheaval in the social structure, or an overall strategy for transformation. These range from fiscal interventions into the superpower of transnational finance (the Tobin tax) to political measures against new patterns of exploitation and welfare retrenchment (the guaranteed basic income), from proposals for audits of odious debt and policies of sovereign default (in the cases of Ecuador and Greece) to the socialisation of pension funds. We can speak of reforms without reformism here in the sense that, for all the declarations that another world is possible, the connection between such measures and a broader horizon of emancipatory social change frequently remains opaque. For most observers, neither the laws of motion of capital nor the collective biography of labouring classes provide the sense of a 'progressive' movement that a reformism could assume and channel into egalitarian and liberatory ends.

Historically, the reproach against reformism was the one that could also be levied theologically against the *katechon*: in restraining the devil you also postpone redemption, indefinitely. Concretely, this took the form of polemics against the *embourgeoisement* of proletarian forces, the biopolitical regimentation of the population under welfare systems, and the division and decomposition of class solidarities by a stratification of privilege, in labour aristocracies co-opted both nationally and internationally. Just as waves of paranoid securitisation have made many nostalgic for classic liberalism, so the current waning of reformism may lead one to hanker after a social-democratic purgatory poised between the hell of capitalism unbound and a heaven never to be stormed. Even worse than being co-opted is becoming simply 'surplus to requirements'.

But capital's relation to its own limits, revealed in crisis and employed by ruling classes to intensify their control over the social product, makes the project of imposing limits to capital appear not just strategically counter-productive, but increasingly utopian, as capital continues to try to emancipate itself even further from the working class. The victories of socialist reformism were always, in the words of Shelley's *A Philosophical View of Reform*, 'trophies of our difficult and incomplete victory, planted on our enemies' land'. But they were also functional to the reproduction of the class relation in ways beneficial to capitalist expansion. Perhaps the ebb of class struggle on a mass scale, with its not insignificant geopolitical context, has considerably eroded the collective intelligence of the capitalist class, no longer schooled by its conflicts with labour to strategise over the long-term. The increasing despair of even the most moderate of our contemporary Keynesians testifies to this.

The reformist hypothesis has long been abandoned by the political class, which can at the very best imagine palliative measures directed at restraining the further degeneration of the status quo, but never at actually presenting a plausible path for public welfare. Crisis management and diminishing returns have replaced the promise of growth and affluence. From the debt-fuelled euphoria that things have never been better to the depressive nostrum that things will never again be as good, in a little over a decade. But the possibilities of reviving, even in a considerably altered guise, a social-democratic reformism, with its reliance on waged work as the crucial mediator of political rights, seem far-fetched. Incapable of thinking the structural determinants of unemployment, together with the principled desirability of a radical diminution of work and the elimination of the compulsion to labour to produce noxious commodities under noxious conditions, the current response to the crisis, including on much of the left, appears to imagine that 'a society founded on work', to quote the Italian constitution, remains the irremovable horizon of our social and economic life. A Fordist nostalgia impedes the elaboration of forms of antagonism pertinent to a situation in which the relation between class and labour, the place of industry, the overall dynamic of accumulation and the international division of labour have mutated drastically from the time of the postwar compact in the capitalist core.

It would be both myopic and moralistic to denounce the spontaneous philosophy of reformism that arises out of today's struggles. Though in the final analysis there is no need to believe in a 'right to work' to struggle against redundancies, nor in the benevolence of state institutions to oppose privatisations, it is also true that the ideologies articulated in and by the institutions at the sharp end of 'austerity' cannot but serve as the initial material from which to fashion a consequent antagonism. In this respect, the struggles in public sectors that have already been intensely subjected to forms of managerialism and competitive discipline, when not extensively privatised, will of necessity be inhabited by a contradictory reformism – at once upholding the 'values' embodied in such institutions and subjecting them to critique, asserting the significance of the 'public' as a domain of relative non-commodification while experiencing the parlous effects of governmental control. Or, defending our trophies, while never forgetting we are on the enemies' land.

The classical prospect of a teleological reformism, and the strategic council of caution and gradualism that accompanied it, alongside now faded visions of progress and affluence, no longer persuade. Luxemburg's objection to Bernstein's notion that capitalism could adapt its way out of crisis by means of credit, the unification of capitals, and the spread of communication appears pretty robust in our age of personal banking and credit default swaps. But the seemingly more sober idea of a reformist *katechon* taming capitalist barbarism, so widespread today, is not any more persuasive for that. It is not simply the case that the balance of forces speak against it; it appears to rely on the prospect of something like a capitalism without capitalism: a durable manner of embedding accumulation, neutralising its tendencies to crisis, and arresting its intensifying exploitation of labour and nature, as well as its expulsion of ever greater swathes of the world into various forms of superfluity.

Contrary to idealist narratives of a mere failure of political will, or an inability of new generations to rein in their disruptive demands and desires, the most progressive framework for channelling and containing the pathologies born of the imperative to accumulate, social democracy, fell victim to the difficulty of maintaining its social compact in a global capitalist environment. Though the specific modes of the restoration of class power were in no way predetermined, it is hard to gainsay the conclusion that in a capitalist system a reformist compromise can only be maintained, temporarily, through a fortunate conjunction of the balance of class forces, the cycle of accumulation, and the specific political strategies of workers' movements and capitalist states. The recognition that capitalism can never be fully domesticated is both painful and important. As Fredric Jameson has noted: 'We must support social democracy because its inevitable failure constitutes the basic lesson, the fundamental pedagogy, of a genuine Left.'[1]

If capitalism in the end can neither be bridled nor tamed, what hope for reformism? In the classic sense, none. Though the spectre of social-democracy haunts every statement and demonstration against current class-based assaults on public services and social welfare, the historical conditions for social democracy are absent. But this is no reason either to repudiate recent movements, in keeping with a sterile purism, or to hold unrelentingly to the discriminating mantra, either revolution or reform. At this juncture, it may be more opportune to identify whether, in the absence of a reformist project, any structural reforms, growing out of and extending defensive struggles, could be formulated.

Almost half a century ago, André Gorz proposed this notion of structural (or non-reformist, or revolutionary) reform, as a way of thinking a non-insurrectionary politics outside of the purview of social-democratic reformism. In *Strategy for Labor*, he asked a question that is still on our agenda: 'Is it possible *from within* – that is to say, without having previously destroyed capitalism – to impose anti-capitalist solutions which will not immediately be incorporated into and subordinated to the system?' Whereas a 'reformist reform is one which subordinates its objectives to the criteria of rationality and practicability of a given system', a 'not necessarily reformist reform is one which is conceived not in terms of what is possible within the framework of a given system and administration, but in view of what should be made possible in terms of human needs and demands'.[2] Though Gorz's talk of 'limiting mechanisms which will restrict or dislocate the power of capital' may recall a view of reform as *katechon*, it is the political meaning of structural or non-reformist reforms that should hold our attention.

To discipline capital is to potentiate labour; a structural reform is 'by definition a reform implemented or controlled by those who demand it'. In other words, what is at stake is the possibility of political re-composition, re-skilling and emancipation which is channelled by reforms whose aim is not merely to restrain a degenerative process or to benefit from a progressive one, but to, at one and the same time, make concrete gains *within* capitalism which permit further movement *against* capitalism. Reformism as *katechon* depends on the pessimistic principle of a piecemeal resistance against an otherwise inevitable catastrophe in permanence; reformism as *telos* depends on the optimistic principle of piecemeal victories that go with the grain of history. A politics of non-reformist reform, or of reforms without reformism, relies instead on a practice, devoid of guarantees, of bringing together the antagonistic needs that grow out of defensive tactics with a broader strategy of federating those struggles that present themselves as barriers raised against capital. Gorz's distinction, between reformist and non-reformist reforms, could thus serve as a heuristic tool for an inventory of current measures, born of struggle, that move beyond the utopia of managing capital towards the investigation of means to counter and sap its power.

NOTE

1. Fredric Jameson, *Valences of the Dialectic* (Verso, 2009), p. 299.
2. André Gorz, 'Strategy for Labor', in S. Larson and B. Nissen, eds., *Theories of the Labor Movement* (Wayne State University Press, 1987), p. 102.

20
Direct Action and Unmediated Struggle

South London Solidarity Federation

If we are to stand any chance of winning the world, we need direct action, self-organisation and solidarity. Jumping through the hoops of representation and the legalism of trade unions and political parties only serves to dilute our struggles and sacrifice our control over them, rendering us passive 'stakeholders' or 'shareholders' in the process. Rather than being spectators in a mediated struggle, we must act for ourselves and represent ourselves.

Our actions are informed by two closely linked aims:

1. The desire to improve our situation in the day-to-day, through struggle and building different social bonds.
2. The need to put an end to the underlying system of social relations, capitalism.

Throughout the history of the movement to end the present state of things, there have been currents that have argued for these goals, and which have sought to make the means and ends of the struggle against capitalism and class society consistent.[1] If we want to effectively engage in class struggle, we need to recapture and revitalise this repressed and neutralised tradition.[2]

When we speak of class struggle, we mean the skirmishes and battles between workers and bosses, oppressors and oppressed, rulers and ruled. The vast majority of the UK's population (indeed, of the world's) are workers. We recognise that there are many divisions between workers based on the amount of power, security and privilege they have, but we don't find the concept of a stable middle class useful. Groups of workers considered middle class a generation ago now find themselves impoverished and under attack. The terms and conditions, to our mind, which marked them out have been salami-sliced away in the last 30 years. So anyone who has to work for a living, or claim benefits, or just scrape by in the margins, is working class.

It is in the interests of all workers to abolish work, by which we mean wage labour. We want freedom, both to govern ourselves and to create new social relations. The ruling classes will not voluntarily give up their power, which is why this change has to be a revolutionary one. The state, which emerged with the purpose of running society in the interests of the ruling class, cannot be turned to another use, such as the administration and re-forging of a free society.[3] Rather it needs to be destroyed along with capitalism and its social and economic hierarchies and institutions.

Anarcho-syndicalism represents our living knowledge of tactics and methods, which have been passed through generations of class struggle. It is the application of anarchist methods to the workers' struggle, through unmediated free association in the places of work/oppression. Key to this is direct action, self-organisation and solidarity. We apply these approaches to everything we do, from building workplace committees, to community organising, to the internal functions of our organisations.

Direct Action is a notion of such clarity, of such self-evident transparency, that merely to speak the words defines and explains them. It means that the working class, in constant rebellion against the existing state of affairs, expects nothing from outside people, powers or forces, but rather creates its own conditions of struggle and looks to itself for its means of action. It means that, against the existing society which recognises only the citizen, rises the producer. And that that producer, having grasped that any social grouping models itself upon its system of production, intends to attack directly the capitalist mode of production in order to transform it, by eliminating the employer and thereby achieving sovereignty in the workshop – the essential condition for the enjoyment of real freedom.

Emile Pouget, *Direct Action*

Most of what the media calls direct action takes the form of spectacular public relations stunts designed to gain attention for a cause that is otherwise fought by legalistic means (i.e. hard lobbying). Direct action, as we know it, is a more immediate tactic which can take many forms: strikes, boycotts, blockades, occupations, pickets, go-slows, sabotage, expropriation and social revolution.[4] The power of direct action lies both in its efficacy and in its immediacy. The anti-poll tax movement demonstrated the strength of direct action, making the tax unworkable and leading to the downfall of Thatcher. Through non-payment and anti-bailiff actions – self-organised solidarity – members of the community were able to resist this attack.

Direct action does not have to be spectacular to succeed. Maintenance workers on the London underground used work to rule (obeying health and safety regulations to minute detail in order to slow down production) to their advantage over a period of several years around the turn of the millennium. Upon hearing of proposed shift increases, workers instituted a so-called 'piss strike'. Every time a worker needed to urinate, they would insist that their Protection Master went with them, leaving the rest of the workers unable to continue without his supervision. Management were shocked by the track workers' suddenly weak bladders and apparent interest in health and safety regulations! Meanwhile, work on the tracks slowed to a snail's pace and management were forced to abandon their plans. Whether in the workplace or in the community, direct action has been employed by the working class for centuries and it is as relevant today as it has ever been.

The ruling class have been using the latest capitalist crisis as an opportunity to attack the working class and the historically accumulated benefits of the liberal welfare state. In response, it has seen an outbreak of mass protests, and, on occasion, economic disruption. This has been both on a small scale, such as protesters storming Town Halls to disrupt council budget meetings, and on the much grander scale of UK Uncut actions, student protests[5] and the autonomous actions on 26 March 2011.[6] It is evident that the new British coalition government were not expecting such a response, given that they are cutting the police as well – a mistake Thatcher never made.

Street demonstrations may not be the most effective form of action but they allow us, and the ruling class, the opportunity to gauge what is the real strength of feeling, to show our colours and meet in solidarity. We cannot, however, demonstrate our way to a better world, nor does being right guarantee us our rights. We know that symbolic demonstrations of opinion, such as against the war in Iraq in 2003, can easily be ignored. We cannot be sure that direct action would have stopped the Iraq invasion, but we can see from the state's response that peace campaigners trying to disrupt military bases was much more threatening than a million people walking from A to B.[7]

The trade unions in Britain have always generally been against using direct action, partly because of their social-democratic mindset, though the anti-strike laws also play a role. There are laws against solidarity in the UK which prevent workers from striking unless they have a trade dispute with their employer and have jumped through hoops designed to let lawyers and big businesses take unions to court for minor infractions. The most militant of the unions, the RMT, regularly has to re-ballot for strikes over technicalities concerning the delivery of ballot papers to a handful of workers, yet even their isolated persistence has led to calls from Conservative politicians and think-tanks to impose tougher restrictions.[8]

In reality, as the 2009 Lindsey oil refineries strike showed, laws can be ignored if you are strong enough and well-organised.[9] Refusing to use direct action is like fighting with one hand tied behind your back, while kowtowing to anti-strike laws takes care of the other hand. Small wonder the unions are more fat-cat than wildcat. For anarcho-syndicalists, strikes are not only vehicles for winning concessions but an opportunity to generalise and weave together resistance and solidarity, en route to our strongest tool: a general strike.

In the Syndicate the members control the organisation – not the bureaucrats controlling the members.

Tom Brown, *Syndicalism*

The Solidarity Federation is not a union, but a revolutionary union initiative which seeks to integrate the economic and the political, the day-to-day struggle and the revolutionary struggle. There is a further difference we should note: the trade unions are tied to a model of representation. They represent their members, at work, and are tied (either formally or informally) to the Labour Party, who allegedly represent the workers' interest in Parliament and local authorities. This is so far removed from reality that only the blindest of leftists still parrot this line. Labour are just another political party supporting big business. However, even if the more militant unions were to shift their support to, say, the Socialist Party, the top-down model, where workers do not control their representatives and cannot recall them, it would continue to inhibit our struggle.

We favour horizontal organisation which provides democratic unmediated structures of social relations. In contrast to the existing union structures, we are building for workers' councils and democratically controlled mass assemblies. If we think we can run the whole world, we ought at least to be able to run our own struggles. This is sometimes called a prefigurative approach, because it mirrors the new world we want to build through our actions in the here and now. This acts as a school of struggle, with participants learning as they go and becoming aware of their own power. Workers who take action start to demystify the processes involved, seeing through the specialisations they are told are necessary – whether of management or union – and start to take that power back.

Self-education leads to self-organisation. Our workplace organiser training provides the tools with which to fight the boss and facilitate bottom-up organising. With the low level of strikes and the halving of union membership in the last two decades, it is evident that militancy needs to be relearned. Some think revolt can happen spontaneously, but whenever you look deeper into a 'spontaneous' action, you find agitators laying the groundwork. Although we accept that for most of the time we are going to be part of a militant minority, we reject the ideas or organisational models of vanguardism. Unlike the trade unions, we are not subject to the anti-strike laws and make a point of inoculation – discussing potential disciplinary procedures and knowing your enemy when planning action.[10] What we can do, at the moment, is support people from outside the workplace, with pickets, leafleting and other forms of pressure.

The prefigurative approach does not preclude bread and butter issues. Rather, it informs how we fight to improve our lives. We reject the idea that day-to-day struggles are somehow subordinate to the struggle for revolution. Standing up for ourselves in our day-to-day lives to improve our quality of life as workers, against racism or sexism, building solidarity and self-organising are all seeds of libertarian communism. In Puerto Real, Spain, community assemblies formed in support of shipyard workers taking industrial action demonstrated the strength of self-organisation. As one CNT member explains, 'every Thursday of every week, in the towns and villages in the area, we had all-village assemblies where anyone connected with the particular issue [of the rationalisation of the shipyards], whether they were actually workers in the shipyard itself, or women or children or grandparents, could go along ... and actually vote and take part in the decision making process of what was going to take place'.[11] With such popular input and support, the shipyard workers won their demands and the assembly continued after the strike of 1987, creating structures 'very different from the kind of structure of political parties, where the decisions are made at the top and they filter down'.[12]

It is necessary to organise the power of the proletariat. But this organisation must be the work of the proletariat itself ... Organise, constantly organise the international militant solidarity of the workers, in every trade and country, and remember that however weak you are as isolated individuals or districts, you will constitute a tremendous, invincible power by means of universal co-operation.

Michael Bakunin

Solidarity is one of our most powerful weapons. When we stand and act together we are stronger than when we act alone. As anarcho-syndicalists, we support each other in our day-to-day struggles and argue for the working class to unite across the divisions and boundaries created or perpetuated by capitalism, such as race, gender, employment status or anything else our rulers use to keep us weak. One of the most effective forms of solidarity is secondary strike action, which is now illegal in Britain. Secondary action consists of striking in support of other workers in struggle, augmenting the stoppage's impact. Striking workers often find themselves ignoring the laws of the ruling class, not because it's fun (although it may well be), but because otherwise they'll lose.

Solidarity is not a matter of sentiment but a fact, cold and impassive as the granite foundations of a skyscraper.
							Eugene V. Debs

With the globalisation of capitalism we have become more vulnerable to attacks. We have to respond in turn with global solidarity. This is already happening to an extent, with groups such as the International Workers' Association taking action in support of its constituent groups and other groups of workers. A recent campaign saw six Serbian anarchists and IWA members, falsely accused of international terrorism, released from prison following worldwide pickets of Serbian embassies and businesses. The concept of solidarity is gaining currency with the burgeoning anti-austerity movement, but it needs to be more than a hashtag. Rather, solidarity must be to the proletarian class like granite to Debs' skyscraper.

We carry a new world here, in our hearts. That world is growing in this minute.
							Buenaventura Durruti

In this moment of crisis and class confrontation the stakes are high and how we fight will affect generations to come, even if we do not win. We see direct action spreading out of necessity. The more that people come to realise the futility of representative politics and moribund trade unionism, the more they will have to look to themselves, their fellow workers and community for solutions. Anarcho-syndicalist groups around the world strive to bring the politics and methods we have described to the class struggle, because these ideas work and that's what counts. There is a rich history and living tradition there for anyone to grasp.

We are trying to revitalise this tradition, building from the bottom up and organising action around our collective grievances in our workplaces and communities. We cannot rely on spontaneous class struggle emerging. We need to be spreading anarcho-syndicalist methods and ideas and creating struggles, however small, that use direct action and bring about improvements in our lives. In time, these struggles will escalate and broaden, with the aim of bringing them together to create a workers' movement capable of challenging capital and state.

NOTES

1. If our aim is libertarian communism, we must organise and act along the principles of this new society in the here and now.
2. See V. Damier, *Anarcho-Syndicalism in the Twentieth Century* (Black Cat Press, 2009).
3. For more on this see R. Rocker, *Anarcho-Syndicalism: Theory and Practice* (AK Press, 2004), pp. 12–14.
4. E. Pouget, *Direct Action* (Kate Sharpley Library, 2003).
5. For more on the student protests and UK uncut actions see D. Hancox, *Fight Back! – A Reader in the Winter of Protest* (openDemocracy, 2011).
6. The TUC-organised march of 26 March 2011 featured an occupation of Fortnum and Mason's and a large black bloc presence.
7. The state happily broke its own laws to detain protesters and stop them passing along a public highway.
8. Policy Exchange made a number of suggestions including that a majority of employees in the balloted workplace vote, a policy endorsed by Boris Johnson, who's election as Mayor of London would have been discounted if the same logic were applied to the electorate. See 'Modernising Industrial Relations', 9 November

2010, http://www.policyexchange.org.uk/publications/category/item/modernising-industrial-relations

9. The Lindsey workers organised unofficial action against attempts by employers to undermine national wage agreements. While there was media controversy about the alleged nationalist content of this dispute, the most important thing for us is that it showed workers can successfully ignore the anti-strike laws if they are strong enough.

10. This means preparing the people involved for the risks, including the worst possible ones, creating support structures and plans for resisting repercussions and victimisation. It is against the law to sack strikers or union organisers, but that does not mean it doesn't happen. In our view, the best defence against it is the solidarity of your colleagues and workmates, not a slow-grinding employment tribunal process whose decisions rarely go in favour of workers and are often ignored when they do.

11. Solidarity Federation, *Anarcho-Syndicalism in Puerto Real: From Shipyard Resistance to Direct Democracy and Community Control* (Theory and Practice, 2011), p. 5.

12. Ibid., p. 6.

Afterword
Rage Against the Rule of Money

John Holloway

This was a year of rage. When the movements in North Africa and the Arab world started at the beginning of 2011 to proclaim Fridays as Days of Rage, days for the concentrated expression of accumulated anger, they set the tone for the whole year: 2011, a year in which rage ran through the world. Arab spring, European summer, American autumn, topped by a global day of rage on 15 October. And now Occupy camps everywhere I go. Dies irae indeed: day of wrath, but with the crucial difference that, unlike the medieval hymn, the anger is not a judgement that comes down from a god on high, but one that is exploding from below, exploding in the streets.

An age of crisis, such as the present, is an age of rage. Crisis is the sharpening of social tensions, of frustrated expectations and the bitterness that grows from that frustration. More and more people cannot find employment and the wage that goes with it. For those that do, the stress and the insecurity is much greater. In October, unemployment among young people stood at 46 per cent in Spain, 43 in Greece, 32 in Ireland, 27 in Italy, 22 in the UK and 24.6 in the United States, with the expectation that it would continue to rise. Many, many young people cannot go to university because they do not have the money to pay for it. More and more people die simply because there is no medical attention available for them. The number of people living in extreme poverty increases. There is more violence, both state and non-state violence. If there is a structural anger permanently built in to the way that society is organised, then this is accentuated in periods of crisis.

And so we rage. And we rage all the more because we do not know what to do with our rage, we do not know how to use our rage to make the world a different place.

We rage against the obvious, against the government. But we know that that there is no answer to be found there. We know, or at least those of us who have lived in democracies know, that representative democracy holds our rage entrapped: like a rat in a maze with no exit we run from one party to another, from one leader to another, from Major to Blair to Brown to Cameron, but there is no way out, things do not get better, cannot get better, because behind all the political power stands another, greater power, the power of capital, the power of money. Berlusconi, Papandreou, Mubarak, Gaddafi, all have fallen in this year of anger, yet the power of money remains.

Finding no hope in the parliamentary parties, we turn to the left, to the revolutionary parties. They articulate the rage loud and clear: fight the Tory scum, they say, fight the cuts, fight for the right to work, defend the NHS, defend the universities. And we shout happily with them. And then we begin to wonder, and to think that the problem is not that the Tories are scum, but that all politicians are scum, simply because their job is to displace us, to take our place. Better, not 'out with the Tories' but 'out with the lot of them' ('*Que Se Vayan Todos*', as the people chanted on the streets of Buenos Aires in 2001). And it is strange to fight for the right to work when we know that the right to work is the right to be exploited, the right to create profits for capital. And what does it mean to simply defend the state when we know that the state is oppressive and bureaucratic and just another part of the system? Our rage against the attacks upon us can easily lead us into defending the system as it exists, but that is not the way we want to go. When capital is in difficulties, it is not for us to defend it or offer solutions but to find a way of jumping upon it.

Our rage keeps running down dead-end streets. But that is dangerous, for we know that it can easily turn bitter, we know that it can lead to domestic violence, to racism, to fascism even. Increasingly, that is what is happening around us. We only have to look back a few months to the English riots to see how ambiguous rage can be. Or look at the attacks on the Christian Copts in Egypt not very long after the Arab Spring. Or the way in which the demonstrations outside the Parliament in Athens turned into fighting between the communists (Communist Party supporters) who wanted to defend the Parliament and the anarchists who wanted to attack it. Or look at the rage of the Tea Party in the United States or the rise of racism throughout Europe in recent years. Or look back at the form that social rage took during the last great crisis of capitalism. Rage can so easily become a rage of hatred and destruction.

We are living in days of rage, and this social rage is likely to continue and intensify in the years that come. It makes no sense to say that it should not be so, that people should be reasonable. The rage is there and growing, and we are part of it. We cannot stand outside it. We are riding on a tiger and we cannot get off. What we can perhaps do is influence the direction in which it moves. That is why it is important to reflect on the object of our rage.

We rage, then, not just against the politicians, not just against the bankers, not just against the rich: we rage against the rule of money.

Not against money, necessarily, because in the present society, no matter how austerely we may (or may not) like to live, we often need money to realise our projects. We rage rather against the rule of money, against a society in which money dominates, in which at every turn money intrudes to determine what is done and what we can do. Money is a great bulldozer tearing up the world around us. Money is an insidious force penetrating ever more aspects of our lives and of our relations with other people. The movement of money is the movement of social disintegration. Money holds society together but it does so in a way that tears it apart.

We used to think that we had pushed the rule of money back decisively. That was perhaps the great hope, achievement and finally myth of the twentieth century. We thought that in a big part of the world, as a result of the Russian, Chinese and other revolutions, money no longer determined social development. And not only that: with the welfare state in many other countries, the rule of money seemed to have been pushed out of areas like health, education and, to a lesser extent, housing. There was a reality in that: the great struggles of the twentieth century really did push back the rule of money in ways that significantly altered the quality of life. To be able to go to the doctor without worrying about money, to be able to send our children to school without worrying about the cost – they are achievements that should not be dismissed, achievements that must be defended where they still exist.

Yet the pushing back of the rule of money was not the breaking of its power that we hoped for. The state seemed to provide the alternative to the rule of money: the rule of the state replaced the rule of money, it seemed, but it did not work like that – for two reasons. Firstly, because the state is a form of organisation based on the administration of society by full-time officials, that systematically excludes people from running their own lives.

But also there is a deeper reason: the rule of money is the rule of labour, of an alienated abstract labour that is imposed upon us. Money is a form of social cohesion, of social nexus, that rebounds upon what we do, how we do it and every detail of our lives. Money shapes our doing but at the same time it is produced and reproduced by the way that we do the things we do. Money transforms our activity, our doing, into labour or, more precisely, into abstract or alienated labour, and it is this abstract labour that produces and reproduces the rule of money. The need for money compels us to spend much of our lives doing things that we do not control and that often have no meaning for us, and at the same time it is this way of behaving that produces a world ruled by money.

The rule of money is the rule of abstract labour: each reinforces the other. The only way of breaking the rule of money (the dynamic of death) is by transforming the activity on which it is based, by breaking abstract labour and replacing it by a different doing, a concrete self-determining activity. But neither the socialist revolutions nor the welfare state did anything at all to break the hold of labour. On the contrary, they strengthened ꓵormously the dominance of labour over alternative forms of activity and so strengthened the rule of money which they apparently sought to undermine.

And so in the last part of the twentieth century, money reappears in all the arrogance of its unbroken power. The great revolutions are swept aside, the welfare state is openly attacked. Money returns in all its violence, driving millions and millions of peasants from the land, transforming the cities of the world into gigantic slums, subjecting all life to the rule of profit, measuring everything. Money, it is proclaimed, is the only legitimate form of social cohesion, the only rational way in which people can come together. Bow down to the rule of money! Abstract labour is the only way of doing, and abstract labour is the rule of faster-faster-faster. Bow down to the rule of money, bow down to the rule of labour!

And on our side? The drive against the rule of money is still there, still the key to our humanity and our hope. And now it is no longer focused on the state: the illusion of the state as the alternative to money has been greatly weakened, though it has not disappeared. Now the drive against the rule of money increasingly takes the form of the creation of interstitial spaces, spaces or moments in which experimental forms of social cohesion are created on a different basis, consciously following a different logic. These are the 'no-go areas' that we saw earlier, the spaces of love, trust or communism that are rooted in everyday life but now push further in an open attack on the rule of money. These can be seen as cracks in the texture of capitalist domination, cracks in the rule of money, moments or spaces that push against-and-beyond existing society.

These cracks come from different directions and often join up, and often do not. They include those forms of solidarity that people develop out of necessity, simply as a way of survival: these have been crucial in the uprising in Latin American cities over the last 20 years, for example. They include too (in a contradictory but very important manner) the struggles to protect what remains of the last great push against the rule of money, the free education, health care and other services provided (albeit inadequately and oppressively) through the state – see for example the current struggles against the cuts in state expenditure in Britain. And thirdly, there are the million initiatives and experiments consciously created outside the structures of the state: the thousands and thousands and thousands of revolts and experiments throughout the world where people are saying 'No, we shall not accept the rule of money, we shall not accept the rule of capital, we shall do things in a different way.' So many refusals-and-creations, so many dignities: sometimes big, sometimes small, sometimes pathetic, always contradictory.

House occupations, social centres, community gardens, alternative radio stations, free software movements, teachers who encourage their students to be critical, doctors who think about their patients and not just about money, peasant rebellions in which the people say 'Enough! Now the people will rule', factory occupations, may day festivals. A world of different refusals-and-creations, a world of dignities. A political economy of resistance, an anti-economy of rebellion, the embryos perhaps of a new world, a world of many worlds.

These cracks are our defence-and-attack against the murderous and suicidal dynamic of the rule of money. These cracks are the only hope that humanity can still have a future. The only hope of creating a radically different world is through the creation, expansion, multiplication and confluence of these cracks, these dignities, these spaces or moments of refusal and creation.

Rage, then, rage against the rule of money. Break the windows of the banks, shoot the politicians, kill the rich, hang the bankers from the lampposts. Certainly all that is very understandable, but it does not help very much. It is money we must kill, not its servants. And the only way to kill money is to create different social cohesions, different ways of coming together, different ways of doing things. Kill money, kill labour. Here, now.

*   *   *

P.S. And now it is January, January of a new year, 2012. The month named after Janus, the god with two faces. Rarely has January been more january, more two-faced. One face looks ˙orward to a year of gloom: of intensifying crisis, more poverty, more starvation, increasing state repression, a more and more desperate struggle by capital to impose the conditions that it needs to ensure its own profitability. This face sees not just an increase of suffering and repression but, even more frightening, a rise of the destructive rage that urges on that repression and closes its ears to the suffering of the world. Yet there is another face, a face that lifts its gaze, a face that rages too, but rages in dignity. This is the face of refusal-and-creation: refusal of the money-attack and, at the same time, the patient and not-so-patient creation of a different world, a world of many worlds, worlds that are not subject to the rule of money. Two antagonistic faces. Which face will predominate? We have no choice. It must be ours. As the rebels in Greece put it: we are not indignant, we are determined.